Reading Michael Balint

Michael Balint is above all known for the 'Balint groups', which came to be a generic term for groups involved with the training of doctors and caregivers in the patient–caregiver relationship. Despite this, the origin and full import of his work has been somewhat overlooked. Hélène Oppenheim-Gluckman provides us with a concise account of how reading Balint has enriched psychoanalytic theory and its practice by broadening the indications for the psychoanalytic cure, the debate on psychotherapies and training of professionals in the caregiver–patient relation.

Reading Michael Balint: A Pragmatic Clinician shows how Balint must be considered as one of the major figures in the British Independent School of psychoanalysis, along with Winnicott and Fairbairn. Oppenheim-Gluckman argues that his ideas, and the implications of his work with groups of medical practitioners, have remained hugely influential within modern psychoanalysis and training in medical psychology.

Reading Michael Balint presents a clear overview of the main tenets of his work. It provides a fresh perspective on Balint's contribution and its importance for modern object-relations theory and practice and brief psychotherapy. It will be an invaluable resource for psychoanalysts, psychoanalytic psychotherapists, counsellors and trainee psychoanalysts and doctors.

Hélène Oppenheim-Gluckman is a psychiatrist and psychoanalyst, and has a doctorate in fundamental psychopathology and practises in Paris. She is a member of the Société de Psychanalyse Freudienne, the Société Médicale Balint, and a Balint group 'leader'. She has published several books and a number of articles in psychoanalytic, medical, psychiatric and political-cultural journals.

'As Hélène Oppenheim-Gluckman tells us in *Reading Michael Balint*, he is above all known for the "Balint groups" and the training of general practitioners in the doctor–patient relationship to help them understand their patients and themselves. As a general practitioner myself, I indeed found the chapters on Balint groups a masterpiece of knowledge and wisdom. But not only were these chapters enlightening for me; reading this book also made me appreciate and easily understand other concepts of Michael Balint, which are all relevant for the practice of any clinician, not only psychoanalysts. I greatly enjoyed reading this book and I felt that I learned a good deal. It also rekindled my enthusiasm for Balint groups. I think and hope that it might do the same for you.'

—*Andre Matalon, Chair of the Department of Family Medicine,*
Rabin Medical Center, Israel; affiliated to the Sackler School of Medicine,
Tel-Aviv University and former President of the Israel Balint Society

'This able and thorough book by Hélène Oppenheim-Gluckman provides valuable insight into Balint's work and its coherence. It still has relevance today for reflection among psychoanalysts confronted with patients who are borderline for the indication of full psychoanalytic cure, coping with the issues arising from psychotherapies, and wishing to develop working relationships with other medical disciplines. Hélène Oppenheim-Gluckman's free-thinking approach will be particularly useful for students in psychology and psychoanalysts in training to enable them to develop their skills and critical abilities.'

—*Patrick Guyomard, Psychoanalyst, Vice-president of*
the Société de Psychanalyse Freudienne
and Emeritus Professor of Psychology in Paris VII University, France

'This is a remarkable book by Hélène Oppenheim-Gluckman, who herself has a longstanding interest and experience in Balint groups in France. She traces carefully Michael Balint's different contributions to analysis, from his Hungarian roots as a disciple of Ferenczi – she discusses Balint's texts, where he leans strongly on Ferenczi – to Balint's developments in all their richness after his emigration in 1939 to England.

As psychoanalysts we might still find Balint's ideas about "primary love", "basic fault", "ocnophils" and "philobats" and "benign" and "malignant" regression useful, although, as Oppenheim-Gluckman writes, they are no longer very well known. Nevertheless some of Balint's case examples seem to be very modern, seen in the light of the "now-moment" (Stern) for instance.

These contributions and Balint's reference to Ferenczi are described and given their full place in the first part of the book, while the second part deals mainly with Balint's work on short-term analytic psychotherapy, developed in the "focal therapy workshop", and his work with general practitioners, the original "Balint groups".

Balint's "workshop", in collaboration with Malan, is the cradle of short-term psychoanalytic psychotherapies, later developed further by others, Klüwer for example, or Luborsky (in German-speaking countries). H. Oppenheim-Gluckman describes the "workshop" and its aims to develop a short-term analytic psychotherapy and to conduct research on it. This also included the development of a technique liable to allow for a sudden and intense moment of understanding between patient and doctor (or nurse, or social worker etc.), the "flash technique".

Then follow the "Balint groups", probably Balint's most fruitful legacy: We follow the development of the first Balint groups, the way they were designed and advertised, and then flourished, and what were the difficulties and deadlocks. H. Oppenheim-Gluckman observes, describes, takes up positions, clarifies.

A refreshing book, which contains historical aspects and the description of Balint's most important ideas.

I recommend it warmly to psychoanalysts or psychoanalysts in training as well as to psychiatrists, teachers, lawyers, doctors in psychosomatic medicine, social workers, nurses and everybody who is interested in the care relationship in caregiving professions.'

> —*Dr. med. Bettina Jesberg, Psychiatrist, Psychosomatic Medicine, Psychoanalyst, Training Analyst DPG, DGPT, IPA; works in her own practice in Berlin, Germany*

'A valuable contribution to the ongoing renewal of interest in Michael Balint. This survey of his writings situates Balint in relation both to Ferenczi and Freud, and to his colleagues in the British Psychoanalytical Society and the Tavistock Clinic. Charting the development of Balint's thought as a psychoanalyst, as a psychiatrist, and as a trainer of doctors and psychotherapists, Hélène Oppenheim-Gluckman provides reference points and a road map, by which to navigate the twists and turns of Balint's multi-faceted work.'

> —*Michael Parsons, member of the British Psychoanalytical Society and French Psychoanalytic Association*

Reading Michael Balint

A Pragmatic Clinician

Hélène Oppenheim-Gluckman

Routledge
Taylor & Francis Group

LONDON AND NEW YORK

First published 2015
by Routledge
27 Church Road, Hove, East Sussex, BN3 2FA

and by Routledge
711 Third Avenue, New York, NY 10017

Routledge is an imprint of the Taylor & Francis Group, an informa business

Previously published in French as *Lire Michael Balint, un clinicien pragmatique*, 2006 by SPS-CP/éditions Campagne Première

British Library Cataloguing in Publication Data
A catalogue record for this book is available from the British Library

Library of Congress Cataloging in Publication Data
Oppenheim-Gluckman, Hélène, author.
  [Lire Michaël Balint. English]
  Reading Michael Balint : a pragmatic clinician / Hélène
  Oppenheim-Gluckman.
    p. ; cm.
  Includes bibliographical references.
  I. Title.
  [DNLM: I. Balint, Michael. 2. Psychoanalysis. 3. Physician-Patient
  Relations. 4. Psychoanalytic Therapy. WM 460]
  RC504
  616.89'17—dc23   2014041817

ISBN: 978-0-415-71378-8 (hbk)
ISBN: 978-0-415-71381-8 (pbk)
ISBN: 978-1-315-71382-3 (ebk)

Typeset in Times New Roman
by Keystroke, Station Road, Codsall, Wolverhampton

Contents

Foreword

The International Balint Federation was set up to promote the work of Michael Balint and the development of Balint groups throughout the world. One important area of our work is the promulgation of literature related to Balint work. To that end we set up a Translation Board to offer financial assistance to translate relevant literature into English. We were delighted to support Hélène Oppenheim-Gluckman's book, the first to be considered by our Board.

In the UK at least, Balint is known chiefly for the concept of Balint groups. Several members of Michael Balint's early groups of general practitioners (GPs) became leading members of the Royal College of General Practitioners and thus helped to introduce Balint's work into the GP curriculum. Although few GPs actually attended Balint groups many of the ideas Balint promulgated have become embedded in the culture of general practice. This, however, has not prevented Balint's work from being misunderstood by many and even derided.

This book undoubtedly helps to set the record straight. Hélène takes us through many of the writings of Balint, so we know what he actually wrote, rather than what we might think (or hope) that he wrote. Such a bibliography would not make for interesting reading. Instead, Hélène links her quotes with a narrative that throws a great deal of light on Balint's work, particularly (for the UK reader at any rate) his work as a psychoanalyst.

When I was a medical student at University College London in the late 1960s, I was privileged to attend the seminars that Balint ran for undergraduates. We students were encouraged by the psychiatry department to attend these seminars but, with a few key exceptions, they were not highly regarded by consultants from other departments. Indeed, Balint became almost paranoid at this lack of support for his work. In 1969 I did a student elective in paediatrics in Paris and was amazed to see a notice advertising a lecture by Balint that was to take place in the lecture theatre of the very hospital in which I was based. I wasn't sure whether I would learn much more from the lecture than I had learnt from the groups but I thought I would go and make up the numbers – such a lecture in the UK would probably have been attended by a mere handful of people. Imagine my amazement to find that the 300-seat lecture theatre was completely full and it was literally standing room only.

I later learnt that support for Balint's work in France has been strong for many years. Indeed one of the most authoritative biographies of Balint was written in French by Michelle Moreau-Ricaud.[1] Hélène's book is a valuable addition to this tradition and we are privileged in the English-speaking world to benefit from a beautifully translated English version. As well as educating English-speaking readers about Balint's important work as a psychoanalyst, we also have a summary of the key aspects of Balint's groups. There may well be surprises for many readers here. Hélène traces the evolution of these groups and shows us all the difficulties and failures as well as the successes. Her book has left me pondering as to whether many of today's groups are a little too comfortable for deep learning to take place. This book presents us all with an ideal opportunity to review our work as Balint group members or leaders and learn again from Michael Balint.

Paul Sackin
General Secretary, International Balint Federation

Note

1 M. Moreau-Ricaud, *Michael Balint: le renouveau de l'école de Budapest* (Ramonville Saint-Agne: Erès, 2000).

Acknowledgements

This book is the result of thirty years of interest in Balint. It would not have been possible without the finely tuned training provided by P. Benoit and M. Sapir, and my work in my first Balint groups alongside C. Brisset and P. Koechlin.

I would like to thank Aurore Cartier and Fanette Martin from the medical library of the Institut Marcel Rivière (Paris) for their very able assistance in the bibliographic research required.

My thanks also to Judith Dupont, who contributed so much to the translation of the works of Balint and Ferenczi enabling them to be better known, and for her bibliographic assistance in the English translation of the present book.

I must also thank Laura Dethiville for her bibliographic assistance in the translation of this book into English and Angela Swaine Verdier for agreeing to take on the translation.

I would like to thank the International Balint Federation. The translation of this book, first published in France by Campagne Première under the title *Lire Michael Balint, un clinicien pragmatique*, would not have been possible without the grant from the International Balint Federation.

Introduction

Michael Balint is best known for his work on training in medical psychology seen in the light of the psychoanalytical approach. However, his work is far more complex and wide-reaching. Reading Balint, whose work is often not familiar to the younger generations of analysts, psychotherapists and physicians, has its usefulness for anyone interested in psychoanalysis, in the training of psychoanalysts and doctors, and in what is generally referred to as the doctor–patient relationship.

There are three ways to approach Balint's work. He is first of all famous for the 'Balint groups', a recognised method for training physicians and caregivers in the doctor–patient relationship. He also sought to further psychoanalytical theory and the practice of cures by widening their indications. He took up position against Freud's theorisations on primary narcissism. He developed a theory of early object relations and pre-oedipal states in psychic functioning, which had consequences for the setting in which psychoanalytical cures took place, on their indications and on psychoanalytical practice more generally. He followed numerous borderline and Psychotic[1] patients. Finally, he was a psychiatrist and psychologist. Some of his work was based on the methods of experimental psychology.[2]

Balint was a disciple of Sandor Ferenczi. He was one of the mainstays of the Hungarian Psychoanalytical Society before emigrating to Britain. This affiliation had considerable influence on his thinking, his itinerary, his practice, his reflection on the training of psychoanalysts and his focus on developing 'brief psychotherapy' methods and training general practitioners in direct contact with patients in the 'psychodynamic' aspects of medical diagnosis.

In Britain, he took part in the debates of the British Psychoanalytical Society, dominated by Ernest Jones and Melanie Klein, but did not relinquish his analytical grounding. There he found recognition, despite the fact that he remained somewhat on the fringe, as he said himself.[3] He however retained his singularity, and did not hesitate to give consideration to the effects of psychoanalysis outside the standard psychoanalytic cure, via research into brief forms of psychotherapy and the doctor–patient–illness relationship. It is probably a dose of pragmatism, his enduring attention to links between theory and practice, his clear awareness of the limitations of psychoanalysis and his ability to think in interdisciplinary terms that gave him an original place within the psychoanalytical movement, and gained recognition for his work in other environments, for instance, among medical doctors. He published several times in the prestigious medical journal *The Lancet*.

In his work, the different lines of research and practice cannot be envisaged in isolation. All his theories about medicine, and the functioning of Balint groups, are based on his theory of archaic functioning modes and early object-relations in the infant. More generally, his work is centred on the question of the primitive object-relation and the corresponding required adjustments to the therapeutic relationship. The medical sphere for him is one of these primary objects, both for the patient and for the doctor. The object-relationship theory occupies an important place in his analysis of transference and counter-transference, in the conduct of 'brief psychotherapies' and in the choice of interpretations.

In the 1960s and the 1970s the impact of Balint's work was considerable in the training of doctors in medical psychology. He was a reference both for psychoanalysts seeking to develop clinical practice in the medical domain linking up with psychoanalysis, and for numerous doctors seeking to enhance their practice by opening up more to the relational aspects of medicine. Balint groups developed across Europe, along with Balint societies which federated at international level. They still exist today, but the practice of Balint groups has declined considerably. Paradoxically, the contributions that Balint made to doctor–patient relationship issues are fully accepted, while their origin is often forgotten. His work has little prominence in the literature today.

Thus reading Balint is to return to the issues that he broached and his theoretical elaborations and bring them into a present-day perspective, so as to show what made him a precursor of today's debates on psychotherapy, the doctor–patient relationship, medical ethics, the training of psychoanalysts, research methods and psychoanalytical clinical practice.

Notes

1 Texts such as M. Balint, 'Contributions to reality testing' in *Problems of Human Pleasure and Behaviour* (New York: Liveright, 1956), pp. 153–70 provide information on his work with psychotic patients.

2 M. Balint, 'Individual differences of behaviour in early infancy and an objective method for recording them' in *Problems of Human Pleasure and Behaviour*, pp. 125–52.
3 In M. Balint, *The Basic Fault* (Evanston, IL: Northwestern University Press, 1992).

Part I

Balint the psychoanalyst

Chapter 1

Balint, a disciple
of S. Ferenczi

Michael Balint was analysed by Sandor Ferenczi, and that inheritance is present in his elaborations. He was his literary executor, and it was he who initiated the publication of his complete works. His death prevented him from completing this work, and it was pursued by others. The exchanges of letters between Balint and Ernest Jones between April 1938 and January 1958[1] show his genuine desire to publish Ferenczi's work, and the obstacles he encountered in achieving this. He provided Ernest Jones with part of the Freud–Ferenczi correspondence, probably with a degree of reluctance. This correspondence was later used by Jones for the drafting of the last volume of the biography of Freud, published in 1957.[2] After this publication, which attributes paranoia to Ferenczi at the end of his life, thus discrediting his last works, Balint published a disclaimer, where he stated his disagreement with Jones, but avoided breaking off completely. This attitude led to criticism from Ferenczi's supporters, who were indignant about what Jones had written. Balint is for instance called an opportunist by Clara Thompson.[3]

Balint devoted several texts to the life and work of Ferenczi.[4] He partly prefaced the French edition of his complete works. He thought it important to circulate the inheritance of Ferenczi to the analyst community, and to have it accepted in spite of the issues with Freud. But Balint's texts on Ferenczi were not only 'political'. Ferenczi's inheritance profoundly influenced his clinical practice and his theories. He was anxious to advocate a relationship to psychoanalysis with which he could identify.

Balint underlines the deleterious aspects of the disagreement between Freud and Ferenczi.[5] Freud wanted nothing to do with the 'active technique' favoured by Ferenczi, and opposed the idea that the analyst, in certain instances, could meet the affective needs of the patient. There were other theoretical disagreements between the two men on the subject of the reality of traumatic events in childhood, and on the theory of early seduction in children. They did not overcome these disagreements, and Balint concluded that this resulted in a trauma for the psychoanalytic community and a sort of theoretical stagnation. In particular, regression viewed as 'a therapeutic ally' was neglected by numerous analysts, and often considered as pathogenic. This situation can be explained by the difficulty that Freud had in giving a meta-psychological status to this concept, which he later linked, in 1920, to the death instinct.[6] For Balint, the conflict between Freud and Ferenczi had several explanations: differing clinical experiences of cases of regression, a somewhat over-hasty generalisation by Ferenczi on the basis of a just a few psychoanalytic cures, despite a readiness to moderate or criticise his own clinical or theoretical positions, and great similarities in character between Freud and Ferenczi, forming a 'tragic friendship'. Balint attempts not to appear as breaking away from Freud, while at the same time positioning himself in line with Ferenczi, and linking this debate to his own theoretical elaborations and to what he was seeking to promote in the analytic community. He broaches the subject explicitly in *The Basic Fault* when he sets out his views on regression and the organisation of the psychoanalytic cure for the purpose of catering for patients with varied pathologies. In this same period, other psychoanalysts in the British Psychoanalytical Society, such as Winnicott, were also working on regression with their own theories, which led Balint to conclude: 'thus, in any case, I am not in bad company'.[7] For Balint, the controversy between Freud and Ferenczi involved several issues: the 'active technique', which Freud only distanced himself from at a later stage, and the way to approach regression in cures with patients who have undergone early trauma, in other words how to respond to a patient in a state of regression and in a situation of intense transference. This second question seemed to him essential, and he considered it should be debated among psychoanalysts. The distinction he makes between 'benign' and 'malignant' forms of regression, the fact that he did not consider regression to be a solely intrapsychic manifestation but also to belong to the early object relation, in his view made it possible to go beyond the debate between Freud and Ferenczi.[8] The text 'Sandor Ferenczi's technical experiments'[9] is enlightening here. It was written late, in 1967, and can be considered as a sort of testament. In this text, Balint analyses the works of Ferenczi as a whole, and his itinerary. He set out to show that Ferenczi did not create a hiatus in psychoanalytical theory, and that he in fact contributed to broadening it.

From the outset, he contrasts Ferenczi with other analysts such as Karl Jung, Alfred Adler and Melanie Klein.[10] Ferenczi, he claims, was constantly searching, and his elaborations do not form a global theory as with other analysts: 'It was always the treatment itself that mattered to him, and never the working out of a tidy system.' Balint in his own career claims a similar pragmatism. Several of Ferenczi's elaborations, he says, are today integral parts of the classic technique, without their origin being identified. A parallel with Balint's own work immediately comes to mind. The same thing occurred, after his death, with his elaborations on the medical sphere. Balint stresses the fact that Ferenczi's work does not fit into any preconceived frame, and that he was known as the *enfant terrible* of psychoanalysis. These are positions that Balint could no doubt claim for himself. Even if he was always integrated into analytic circles, because of his research and his theoretical stances, he occupied a marginal position and was often criticised by colleagues. His aim was to open psychoanalysis to new areas, and he frequently deplored the weight of theories that he considered too rigid and too restrictive.[11] Although towards the end of his life he was President of the British Psychoanalytical Society, despite the decisive influence of Jones and Klein, he always saw himself 'in the group which belongs merely to the fringe'.[12] In 'The disagreement between Freud and Ferenczi, and its repercussions', he writes:

> The general impression, thus, is that of bleakness and stagnation [in the British Psychoanalytical Society]. Still, in recent years there have been a few analysts, admittedly very few, who were interested in the problem of therapeutic regression. . . . All these analysts, including myself, belong – not to the 'classical' massive centre – but to the fringe. *We are known, tolerated, perhaps even read, but certainly not quoted.*[13] (My emphasis)

Several times in the text Balint uses the phrase '*enfant terrible* of psycho-analysis' which he attributes to Ferenczi.[14] This epithet, according to Balint, concentrates aspects of Ferenczi's personality, theoretical issues and the controversy generated by his work, and these three aspects are linked. In 'Dr Sandor Ferenczi as psychoanalyst',[15] Balint writes:

> He could not bear empty formulas and pompous pretentious learnedness; on the contrary, he prized above all concrete clinical observations and a thorough examination of the condition of the patient. The academicians of our science did not like him, they feared his *élan* and regarded him as an *enfant terrible*. Ferenczi took note of this nickname with a bitter smile; it hurt him, but also made him feel proud. He felt that he was not understood, that mutual misunderstanding, the 'confusion of tongues'[16] surrounded even him, who had devoted his life's work to the removal of this confusion between the child and the grown-ups, between the patient and his analyst.

And in a text published fifteen years later[17] Balint writes:

> During all the years I knew him, he used to joke about being the *enfant terrible* of psycho-analysis. He was proud of this position, but it was a bitter pride. His favourite story, quoted by him on innumerable occasions, in dignified scientific discussions as well as at gay social parties, was the

fantasy of the 'wise baby'[18] who, though still in the cradle, is wiser than the whole family, wiser, in fact than all the grown-ups put together. . . . The analysis of such dreams and fantasies proves, however – as Ferenczi himself told us – that this wisdom was bought at a heavy price indeed; a desperate effort inevitably bound to fail. In reality . . . children remain children, however wise; they can only play at being, but never in childhood really be, adults. I think this was the insurmountable barrier that separated Ferenczi from his colleagues. Freud and Abraham were essentially mature adults. Ferenczi, in spite of his profound insight, his many-sided talents, his unsurpassed qualities as a clinical observer, and his unbounded scientific fantasy, was essentially a child all his life.

Ferenczi and the psychoanalytic technique

In 'Sandor Ferenczi's technical experiments', several points in Ferenczi's work appear important to Balint: the therapeutic value of regression in the analytic situation; the importance of the interpretation of transference; the place given to counter-transference (the Balint groups are mainly centred on counter-transference by the physician); the danger of repetition of early trauma if the analyst is in an over-passive or over-neutral position (Balint strongly emphasises the importance of the 'atmosphere' of the analytic situation or the consultation, or its 'climate', which relates to both verbal and non-verbal elements); and finally the scope afforded by all these elements for providing care for more numerous patients with varied pathologies (a large part of Balint's work derives from this concern).

In line with Ferenczi, Balint considers that the notions of care, of 'gratification' of patients' needs, and of assistance are essential, and should be viewed as such by psychoanalysts. The epithet that would best suit Ferenczi is that of the 'physician'. Balint also describes him as 'the haven of lost cases'.[19] As for Winnicott, the phantasmatic position occupied by the analyst is likened to maternal care. The psychoanalyst:

> is no longer the powerful protector . . . he has become the well-meaning motherly, tender, understanding companion with whom it is possible for the patient to live through the painful events of early life, in order to find jointly with him new and healthier solutions for the mental conflicts which gave rise to the illness.[20]

Thus there is another notion underpinning the therapeutic objectives pursued, that of freedom. 'It was Ferenczi who added to the hitherto prevailing definitions of the final aim of the treatment (overcoming of resistances and removal of infantile amnesia) the new task of teaching the patient how to associate really freely.'[21] This aspect of psychoanalysis, both pedagogical and ethical, is one of Balint's main concerns.

The text 'Sandor Ferenczi's technical experiments' is divided into three parts, reflecting three theoretical periods: 'Contribution to classical technique', the 'Active technique' and 'Pointers to future developments'. In each of these sections, Balint quotes and comments on Ferenczi's texts and on a few texts by Freud.

Contribution to classical technique

Several articles by Ferenczi characterise this first period. In chronological order, 'On obscene words', 'Washing-compulsion and masturbation', 'The dream of the "clever baby"' and 'The problem of acceptance of unpleasant ideas'.[22]

The article 'On obscene words' was written in 1911. Following on from Freud,[23] it broaches the subject of the function of obscene words for patients, and their importance in relation to repressed childhood complexes. Balint's interest for this text resides in several points that are encountered in different forms throughout Ferenczi's work. First, Ferenczi is interested in language, and specifically in the words that can be used by the psychoanalyst when addressing the patient. The obscene word, he considers, 'possesses the capacity of compelling the hearer to revive memory pictures in a regressive and hallucinatory manner'. It has a tangible, sensory, concrete nature and is linked to the first phases of development of the individual, unlike other words that are linked to more abstract thought appearing in later stages of development. The particular features of the language used by the patient and the analyst when dealing with regression phases in the course of a cure, and the fact that an 'adult language' used by the psychoanalyst is unsuitable at such times, led to numerous elaborations by Balint.[24] Second, Ferenczi attaches considerable importance to transference and counter-transference. Using obscene words arouses resistance in both the patient and the analyst. Ferenczi's attention to the analyst's counter-transference, and the resistance he perceives in himself when the question of the obscene word is raised in the cure, led him to elaborate on this issue. Here, what interests Balint is the attention paid by Ferenczi to the smallest detail of the session in relation to its 'atmosphere'. This word, very often used by Balint in his accounts of psychoanalytic cures or psychotherapies, and in his work on the medical sphere, is linked to the attention paid to 'pre-verbal' material, and the quality of the interaction between the patient and the analyst or caregiver. The word is, however, not well defined. In *The Basic Fault* he writes:

> Object relationship is always an interaction between at least two people and, more often than not, is created and maintained also by non-verbal

means. It is difficult to find words to describe what it is that is created. We talk about behaviour, climate, atmosphere etc. all of which are vague and hazy words, referring to something with no firm boundaries and thus reminiscent of those describing primary substances.[25]

'The dream of the "clever baby"' is a very short text which is a precursor to two other major articles, 'Confusion of tongues between adults and the child' and 'Child-analysis in the analysis of adults'.[26] The central idea of this text, that too much knowledge and wisdom conceals profound distress in the infant and a lack of adaptation of his entourage to his needs, in fact makes it a precursor of Winnicott's theories on 'the false self'. The false self is an outward adaptation to the environment as a mode of defence against 'threats of annihilation', and it is linked to an ego that is 'split off' or 'disintegrated' as a result of an unsuitable environment in the first moments of life.[27] Balint did a lot of work on the unsuitability of environment to the needs of the infant, and on the inappropriateness of the 'adult language' used by analysts with patients in a state of regression. This language takes no account of the patient's situation, and is just as unsuitable as that of the mother in early childhood, but the patient has to adopt it in artificial manner.[28]

What interests Balint is the attention paid by Ferenczi to what he calls 'formal elements', and 'the pervading mood of the associations'. Ferenczi's article 'Dirigible dreams'[29] is an introduction to the psychopathology of daily life, and the same applies to another very important article according to Balint, 'Transitory symptom construction during the analysis'.[30] This second article, which prefigures the 'active technique', is innovatory because of the attention paid by Ferenczi to symptoms appearing in the course of sessions, whether bodily, hallucinatory or obsessional. Ferenczi considered that they cast light on the way in which neurotic symptoms generally form and disappear. If they are well-handled they help the patient to experience the interpretation 'in his own body', so as to generate a 'conviction'. For Balint, they belong to the sphere of transference, and vary in relation to it. They have the status of 'free associations' and a therapeutic function, so long as the therapist does not view them as 'acting-out'. Ferenczi appears as the source of Balint's elaborations first on 'the patient's offers and the Doctor's responses', and second on what he calls the 'drug "doctor"', two key concepts for Balint.[31] This notion of the 'drug "doctor"' reflects the way in which the doctor 'prescribes himself' as an object. When Balint talks of the patient's offer and the doctor's response to it, he is referring to functional somatic disturbances that are appeals to the doctor by the patient. The way they evolve is linked to the response of the doctor, and to the way in which he 'prescribes' himself.

This is the idea that there is no unconscious psychic process that is not contained in the intersubjective relationship, even in the state of narcissistic regression of dreaming,[32] which is also what interests Balint when he quotes a very short article 'To whom does one relate one's dreams?',[33] in which Ferenczi quotes Lessing's epigram: *Alba sibi dormit; somnia alba mihi –* Alba sleeps for herself; Alba dreams for me.

The article 'On the technique of psychoanalysis',[34] a 'typical Ferenczi paper' according to Balint, is a determining text in the work of Ferenczi. Like 'Technical difficulties in the analysis of cases of hysteria',[35] it is an introduction to the 'active technique'. Balint was clearly influenced by three theoretical lines of thought that run through these articles: first, a criticism of free associations, often seen as a sovereign method, or else used too rigidly (in certain patients, such as obsessive patients, resistances interfere with the fundamental rule); second, attention to apparent progress in symptoms, while in fact this may be merely the effect of suggestion linked to transference; and third, the dead ends occurring in the analysis on account of counter-transference by the analyst, and the need for him to constantly work both on his own unconscious and on that of his patient, with 'freedom and uninhibited mobility of psychic excitation'. When commenting on this article, Balint stresses the need for the analyst to be attentive not only to the content of free associations, but also to their form and function for the patient. In several texts[36] he specifies at what moments in the psychoanalytic cure the verbal material, the interpretations of the analyst, and the free associations of the patient are relevant, and at what moment in regression they are not, or may even be factors of resistance or pseudo-adaptation by the patient to what he perceives of his analyst.

The 'active technique'

Balint does not abstain from criticism of the 'active technique'. But his concern is to show the filiation between Freud and Ferenczi on the one hand, and Ferenczi's ability for self-criticism on the other. Ferenczi, at times when the analysis was stagnating, used injunctions or prohibitions to reactivate the process, to bring repressed material to light and to favour the emergence of new associations.

Balint gives considerable attention to two articles by Freud, 'From the history of an infantile neurosis' and 'Lines of advance in psychoanalytic therapy'. The choice of these texts is the fruit of considerable reflection.

He quotes 'From the history of an infantile neurosis'[37] because the end of treatment was fixed by Freud in the case of the 'Wolf-man', as in that reported by Ferenczi in 'Technical difficulties in the analysis of a case of hysteria'.[38] This termination can therefore qualify as an 'active technique'. But he may well also have chosen this text on account of other issues in the debate between Freud and Ferenczi. Freud was against the idea that the analyst might meet the affective needs of the patient when the patient was in regression and had undergone early traumas. Balint probably knew of the particular problems in the case of the Wolf-man, and the fact that the patient was assisted financially by different analysts, and even, on several occasions, by collections that they organised.[39] He, however, says nothing on this score.

Freud's text 'Lines of advance in psychoanalytic therapy'[40] was written in 1919 following a lecture to the 5th Psychoanalytic Conference in Budapest, the same year as the publication of 'On the technique of psychoanalysis'.[41] It is probably cited by Balint for political reasons. Apart from the place where the conference was held,[42] in this text Freud explicitly refers to Ferenczi's 'active technique' as an example to be followed. But the content of the text also interests Balint because Freud proposes to revise certain therapeutic data. It is not enough to evidence resistances in a patient in order to overcome them. There may be a need for 'activity' on the part of the analyst in certain cures, for maintaining a state of frustration or even abstinence – 'analytic treatment should be carried through, as far as is possible, under privation – in a state of abstinence'. The position of the analyst proposed here is highly educative, or even controlling. Referring to the patient's 'divergent paths' in the face of the psychoanalytic treatment, Freud writes: 'It is the analyst's task to detect these divergent paths and *to require* the patient every time to abandon them, however harmless the activity which leads to satisfaction may be in itself' (my emphasis). Further on:

> We cannot avoid taking some patients for treatment who are so helpless and incapable of ordinary life that for them *one has to combine analytic with educative influence; and even with the majority occasions now and then arise in which the physician is bound to take up the position of teacher and mentor.* (My emphasis)

He also proposes to 'put the patient into the mental situation most favourable to the solution of the conflict', and this is taken up by Ferenczi in 'Technical difficulties in the analysis of a case of hysteria', and further developed in 'The further development of an active therapy in psychoanalysis'.[43] This type of approach is used today with other theoretical references in behavioural therapies. Balint does not criticise Freud's positions, but he partly distances himself by stressing the fact that, following on from Ferenczi, the active technique is above all designed to elicit an active position by the patient. Balint is also interested in Freud's text because it recognises that the techniques used by psychoanalysts at the time are suitable for hysteria, but not for other pathologies. Towards the end of this text, Freud anticipates, and refers to a time in the future when psychoanalysis will be applied to a wide population, and when it will be necessary to 'alloy the pure gold of analysis freely with the copper of direct suggestion'. This passage links up with Balint's concerns: that the indications of the psychoanalytic cure should not be restricted to neurotic subjects, and that psychoanalysts should find psychotherapeutic techniques that can be used on a large scale, creating the conditions for 'psychotherapy for the broad masses'.[44] Unlike Freud, Balint wanted to avoid techniques that used suggestion. He positions himself in the follow-on from Ferenczi, who emphasised the risk of alienation of the patient in case of suggestion or hypnosis.[45] When he quotes the end of Freud's article in 'The classical technique and its limitations',[46] he is making use of a text by the founding father of psychoanalysis in his debate with the psychoanalytic community. He criticises psychoanalysts who select patients according to 'analysability' criteria, and who, in the cure, remain on the oedipal level, without attempting to reach pre-oedipal levels. He also asks a fundamental question: who will take care of the other patients, those who are not neurotic? Psychoanalysis, he says, cannot desert the field, as was the case for group psychotherapy. The risk must be taken to launch out into the pre-oedipal levels, and adapt the analytic technique. It is possible to explore new fields without undermining the essential foundation of psychoanalysis. It can but enrich psychoanalytic theory, and rid it of its dogmatic and excessive aspects. He writes:

> Pure gold has the remarkable quality of withstanding any fire and even of being purified by it. I do not see any reason why we should be afraid for the essential parts of our science; and should any of its minor frills burn away, being not of pure gold, the better for future generations.

Unlike what Freud suggests, he considers that there is no confusion between the psychoanalytic position and the educative position, nor between the psychoanalytic position and suggestion or hypnosis once one draws away from the classic field of cures for neurosis.

In addition to 'Technical difficulties in the analysis of a case of hysteria', Balint uses four texts to comment on Ferenczi's ideas on the active technique. The fifth text that he quotes, *The Development of Psychoanalysis*,[47] was written by Ferenczi in collaboration with Rank. 'The further development of an active therapy in psychoanalysis'[48] describes several elements in the active technique. Ferenczi, like Freud, is in favour of maintaining abstinence and privation.[49] The activity is seen as being on the side of the patient who is given a particular task. 'In the cases of phobia the task consisted in the carrying out of painful activities'. The directives of the psychoanalyst 'are not a priori directed to morality, but only against the pleasure principle'. This technique is an educational complement to analysis, and the psychoanalyst can be considered as 'educating the Ego'. This phrase is ambiguous, in particular since the development of 'ego psychology'. Its boundaries with suggestion are unclear, and it assumes that the analyst is in control. Balint returns to the question of pedagogical aspects in psychoanalysis in an article in 1938, 'Strength of the ego and ego-pedagogy'.[50] He differentiates himself from Ferenczi by distinguishing the 'education of the Ego', which may be necessary in the conduct of a cure, and 'education of the Super-ego' which is in contradiction with the purposes of treatment. This distinction, says Balint, means that 'we need no longer be afraid of analysis degenerating into pedagogy'. Balint is cautious in his criticism of aspects relating to authority,[51] control and suggestion in Ferenczi's writings.[52] He prefers to expand on his own viewpoint. The symptoms that arise during a cure, or that do not alter in spite of treatment, the shift of unconscious fantasies towards bodily gratifications, which according to Ferenczi justify the use of the active technique, are for Balint the expression of a 'crisis in the transference relationship'[53] that needs to be specifically taken into account. This concept is found throughout Balint's work. It is one of the main orientations of work in Balint groups.[54] Balint also differentiates himself from the Ferenczi of this period (and from Freud) when he states that the analyst can lean towards frustration (in the case of genital material) but that it is important to also be able to encourage the patient to give himself pleasure freely and openly.[55] From Ferenczi's article 'Psychoanalysis of sexual habits'[56] he notes above all the attention paid to the pre-genital level, on which he did a lot of work. By stressing the need for the patient to be active, and by quoting a note from this article where Ferenczi tempers the extent of his injunctions and prohibitions, Balint seeks to make Ferenczi's assertions more amenable, and to avoid criticising him outright.

The text 'Contra-indications to the active psychoanalytical technique'[57] signals the end of the active technique period. Ferenczi criticises the technique: it increases resistances, it can disrupt or even destroy the transference. There is a risk of drifting towards techniques of suggestion and authoritarian measures that could constitute a traumatic repetition of the parent–child relationship, or of adult sadism towards the patient when he was a child. It remains a possibility, but it should be flexible. Ferenczi also criticises the fixing of an end to the cure by the psychoanalyst, because it can be traumatic. In two articles written in 1949,[58] Balint describes relapses that occur when the end of treatment is fixed in an arbitrary manner. Ferenczi also states that the doctor–patient relationship is the pivot of the analytic material, and that each dream, each gesture, each parapraxis, and any deterioration or improvement in the patient are expressions of the transference relationship and of resistance. Balint clearly identified with these positions.

The book by Ferenczi and Rank[59] in 1924, two years before 'Contra-indications to the active psychoanalytical technique', enabled Balint to identify more easily with Ferenczi. It contains a criticism of the active technique, alongside reflection on the importance of manifestations of transference and counter-transference, and of primitive and archaic object relations. Ferenczi and Rank, criticising over-systematic interpretations that can take on the status of formal knowledge, leading to an identification of the patient with the analyst and changing nothing in his libidinal attitude, give considerable importance to the analytical setting as a whole, and to the role of repetition. This certainly had an influence on Balint. For him, the organisation of the cure should allow for the existence of repetition and regression. He also describes clinical situations where interpretation had no effect because the regression in the here-and-now situation of the session had not been dealt with. He likewise describes situations where patients adopt the language of their analyst, with the attendant therapeutic deadlock and the risk of submission or alienation.[60]

Pointers to future developments

Balint comments on texts published by Ferenczi between 1927 and 1933. They concern his most important technical experiments, because they address the issue of 'the primitive nature of patients' reactions', and 'what the patient might expect from his analyst'.[61] This restores his connections with Ferenczi.

Three articles written in 1928 show a theoretical turning-point for Ferenczi: 'The adaptation of the family to the child', 'The problem of the termination of the analysis' and 'The elasticity of psycho-analytic technique'.[62]

In 'The problem of the termination of the analysis', for Ferenczi, 'no case of hysteria could be regarded as cleared up so long as a reconstruction, in the sense of a rigid separation of reality and fantasy, had not been carried out . . . a neurotic cannot be regarded as cured if he has not given up pleasure in unconscious fantasy, i.e. unconscious mendacity'. The analysis 'is to be a true re-education', so as to create a better adapted personality. This normative ideal, and the notion that we might have control over our unconscious, contradicts numerous analytical theories, and Freud voiced strong criticism.[63] The positions of Balint[64] on the criteria for ending an analysis also reflect an ideal of normality, which however differs from that of Ferenczi: it is the ability of the patient to acquire 'mature genitality' and to develop an active, and not solely passive, object relation, that is to say an ability to love, an ability for empathy and an ability to make allowances for others. However, Balint joins Ferenczi in underlining that the analyst is confronted with the child in the patient, a 'naughty, defiant child' who reveals his hidden needs for tenderness and love, and stressing that there is a need to accept the slow pace of the patient, without artificial interruption. Ferenczi thinks that few analyses are actually completed. In the article 'On the termination of analysis',[65] Balint considers that according to the criteria he has set out, only two out of ten cures are actually complete. This issue is still fully relevant today.

'The elasticity of the psychoanalytic technique' marks a turning-point in Ferenczi's work in relation to the active technique and the finalities of psychoanalysis. Several remarks are important concerning this text. Whether or not to communicate an interpretation to a patient is above all 'a question of tact', and 'capacity for empathy'. Thus the interpretation occurs in a mutual and empathetic object relation between the analyst and the patient, even if not on the same level for each. This relationship is often more important than the interpretation itself. The analyst should be 'sparing with interpretations'. 'Analysis should be regarded as a process of fluid development, unfolding itself before our eyes, rather than as a structure with a design pre-imposed upon it by an architect'. These remarks may have fuelled those made by Winnicott on psychoanalytic work:

> The analyst lets the patient set the pace and he does the next best thing to letting the patient decide when to come and go, in that he fixes the time and the length of the session, and sticks to the time that he has fixed . . . the analyst is always groping, seeking his way among the mass of material offered and trying to find out what, at the moment, is the shape and form of the thing which he has to offer to the patient, that which he calls the interpretation.[66]

'The unobtrusive analyst'[67] by Balint is also related to the text by Ferenczi when he describes how the analyst should adapt to a patient in a state of regression, and how he sometimes has the function of a 'provider of time and of milieu', the aim of the analysis being that the patient 'should be able to find himself, to accept himself, and to get on with himself . . . moreover, he must be allowed to discover his way to the world of objects and not be shown the "right" way by some profound or correct interpretation'. The cure, according to Ferenczi, is a 'bold experiment' for the patient and the psychoanalyst.[68] The controlling, adaptive and educative aspects of Ferenczi's earlier texts have disappeared. The analyst also learns from the patient, and Balint stresses this point. The analyst's mind 'swings continuously between empathy, self-observation, and making judgements'. 'His cathexes oscillate between identification (analytic object-love) on the one hand and self-control or intellectual activity on the other.' This sketching-out of a 'metapsychology of the analyst's mental processes' was used by Balint to support his reflection on the position of the analyst in the cure, and on the work on the unconscious processes in the doctor in Balint groups. The place given to 'working-through' experiences during the cure is once again returned to by Ferenczi. The removal of repression and the emergence of memories or repetition mechanisms in the transferences, even once interpreted, are not sufficient for the patient to progress. One important element in any progression is indeed this working-through. Balint also enlarges on this subject in 'The final goal of psycho-analytic treatment'.[69] He again identifies with aims of analysis as set out by Ferenczi: the need to exercise 'analytic self-knowledge and self-control when necessary', which 'in no way hampers free enjoyment of life', and to possess psychic 'elasticity'. He also appreciates the ability that Ferenczi shows for self-criticism, and the fact that he reappraises the setting of analyses so as to enable the childhood trauma experienced by the patient to be overcome.

'Child-analysis and the analysis of adults'[70] is a very important text by Ferenczi, which probably greatly inspired Balint. Here Ferenczi states that at certain moments in the analysis there is no difference between child and adult analysis.[71] Pre-oedipal, traumatic, infantile material can arise in the course of a session, and be enacted by the patient, and the analyst then uses language and play that is close to those used by child psychoanalysts. For Balint 'adult conventional language' is not suitable for patients in a state of regression. Ferenczi explores the therapeutic use of regression by generating material sometimes in the form of acts and returned to in a here-and-now dialogue in the cure, sometimes converted into a game (play analysis). Balint reports cures with patients in a state of regression where he leaves ample room for body movement during the session, and where these movements are viewed by the analyst as pre-verbal material, and a form of communication directed towards the analyst.[72] He pays particular attention to the here-and-now of the cure or the doctor–patient relationship.

However Balint does not enlarge upon Ferenczi's theories concerning the 'narcissistic split of the self', despite their importance. In certain analytic situations where, in transference, the patient feels abandoned as in childhood (with the attendant risk of 'psychical' trauma), there is, according to Ferenczi, a 'narcissistic split of the self'. This enables self-preservation in the face of intense trauma, by way of a 'splitting' mechanism that can take on different forms. In certain cases 'part of the self splits off and becomes a psychic instance of self-observing'. 'Part of the self' is used for self-help. Ferenczi, in 'Child-analysis and the analysis of adults', thus cites the case of a patient who 'plays by himself':

> Part of the person adopts the role of father or mother in relation to the rest, thereby undoing, as it were, the fact of being left deserted. In this play, various parts of the body – hands, fingers, feet, genitals, head, nose, or eye – become representatives of the whole person, in relation to which all the vicissitudes of the subject's own tragedy are enacted and then worked out to a reconciliatory conclusion.

In other cases there can be a displacement to a single part of the body, enabling the rest to be spared. Referring to a patient in a comatose state during the session as a result of the reliving of intense mental trauma in childhood, Ferenczi writes:

A patient awoke from a traumatic coma with one hand insensible and pallid like a corpse's; otherwise, except for the amnesia, he was fairly composed and almost at a stroke became fit to work. It was not difficult to catch in the very act, as it were, the displacement of all his suffering and even of death on to a particular part of the body: the corpse-like hand represented the whole agonized person and the outcome of his struggle in insensibility and death.

By concentrating on the hand as a representation of the whole person, the subject spares the rest of himself. At the same time, there is abandonment of certain parts of the body, taken over by death. These could be locations of somatic vulnerability and sometimes catastrophic medical complications, on which Balint worked. Thus his lack of interest in this concept is surprising. Is it due to the fact that he elaborated very little on the specific clinical presentation of psychic trauma, even if the question of non-adaptation of the environment to the needs of the infant underpins his reflection? The article 'Trauma and object relationship'[73] is above all intended to clarify the debate between Freud and Ferenczi.

In 'Confusions of tongues between adult and child'[74] Ferenczi devotes a lot of attention to the risk of psychic trauma as a result of 'incestuous seduction' or 'perversion' of the adult. He describes phenomena of identification with the aggressor ('introjection of the aggressor'). Balint returns to these theories in 'Character analysis and new beginning',[75] but not to this last point, again probably on account of the limitations of his elaborations on trauma. A certain number of points considered particularly important by Balint are re-stated in Ferenczi's text. The neutrality of the analyst can be traumatic. When the analyst is confronted with a patient in a state of regression, some of his needs require a response. Conventional adult language is sometimes non-operative. There is a need to shake off all 'professional hypocrisy' towards the patient. There should be no hesitation in making certain gestures. In 'Character analysis and new beginning',[76] Balint cites a case where he held a female patient's finger.

Ferenczi and the medical sphere

Curiously, Balint, in 'Sandor Ferenczi's technical experiments', does not quote Ferenczi on the medical sphere. Yet as soon as the polyclinic in Budapest opened, initiated by Ferenczi, Balint opened seminars for doctors, with the idea of contributing to their training in the area of psychoanalysis.[77] The intention was above all to raise awareness among general practitioners by way of theoretical instruction. He followed on in this from Ferenczi, who had given several lectures to medical societies.[78] Ferenczi wanted to make general practitioners aware of the contributions of psychoanalysis (transference, repression, symptom formation etc.), and to give it 'the important role' it should have in everyday life,[79] in particular in the education of children, prophylaxis for neuroses and awareness of the psycho-genesis of certain somatic illnesses. He suggested that sanatorium teams caring for patients with pulmonary diseases should compulsorily include a psychoanalyst, which in 1923 was a revolutionary proposal. In another text dating from 1933, a short while before his death, Ferenczi stresses the considerable contributions of psychoanalysis to medicine, because it enables unconscious psychic factors to be taken into account in illnesses, and treatment of the patient at the same time as the illness, a principle in medicine that is often not well complied with for lack of authentic psychological knowledge.[80] In an article entitled 'Brief presentation of psychoanalysis' (no English translation),[81] published after his death, he returns to the theme of 'psychoanalysis to serve the general practitioner'. In any medical treatment, one component is the way in which the doctor 'prescribes himself'. However, he adds, 'the Faculty does not tell us how to dose this medication, nor what are its modes of action',[82] while psychoanalysis provides precise knowledge and well-defined methods on this question.[83] What Balint's work owes to these texts is obvious.

Thalassa

In 'Sandor Ferenczi's technical experiments', Balint does not quote Ferenczi's text *Thalassa*[84] either, despite the fact that it clearly provided inspiration for his work. In 'Psychosexual parallels to the fundamental law of biogenetics'[85] written in 1930, he sets out hypotheses concerning human sexuality – that the psychosexual evolution of humans, both bodily and psychic, reiterates phylogenesis – basing himself on Freud, but most of all on Ferenczi. On the *Thalassa* model (which integrates psychoanalysis and biology, creates a 'bioanalysis' and claims the existence of a tendency to regression governing both psychic and organic life), Balint uses a biological model to sketch out his notion of the 'new beginning' that is so important in his theory on regression: 'the organism regresses to an earlier stage of evolution, returning to long-abandoned life-forms, in order to begin its existence anew from there. This *new beginning plays a very important part in the living world*' (original emphasis). His conclusion, that any evolution is paid for by a regression, but that this regression does not necessarily impoverish the world, lays the way for his later elaborations. Likewise, his theory on 'primary object-love' and 'primary substances', corresponding to phases without conflict, are explicitly based on Ferenczi's hypothesis of an initial idyllic state, both phylogenetic and ontogenetic (being in the ocean and in the maternal body), where humans seek to return for the purpose of retrieving primitive object relations rooted in the biological world.

Notes

1 'Correspondence Jones–Balint', *Le Coq Héron* 177 (2004): 25–88. This text was not published in English, only in Hungarian and French.
2 E. Jones, *The Life and Work of Sigmund Freud: Vol. 3: The Last Phase: 1919–1939* (London and New York: Basic Books, 1957).
3 In her letter to E. Fromm dated 5 November 1957 in 'Correspondence Jones–Balint', pp. 94–5.
4 M. Balint, 'Dr Sandor Ferenczi as psychoanalyst' (1933) and 'Sandor Ferenczi' (1948) in *Problems of Human Pleasure and Behaviour* (New York: Liveright, 1956), pp. 235–42 and pp. 243–50; M. Balint, 'The disagreement between Freud and Ferenczi, and its repercussions' in *The Basic Fault: Therapeutic Aspects of Regression* (Evanston, IL: Northwestern University Press, 1992), pp. 149–58; M. Balint, 'Sandor Ferenczi's technical experiments' in B. B. Wolman (ed.) *Psychoanalytic Techniques* (New York: Basic Books, 1967), pp. 147–67.
5 These aspects are explicitly discussed in texts appearing in Balint, *The Basic Fault*: 'Freud and the idea of regression', pp. 119–26 and 'The disagreement between Freud and Ferenczi, and its repercussions', pp. 149–58.
6 S. Freud, 'Introductory lectures on psychoanalysis', *Standard Edition*, Vols XV and XVI (London: Hogarth Press, 1961 and 1963); S. Freud, 'Beyond the pleasure principle', *Standard Edition*, Vol. XVIII (London: Hogarth Press, 1955), pp. 7–66.
7 'Summary' in Balint, *The Basic Fault*, p. 29.
8 Balint's theories on benign and malignant regression and how they should be handled in cures are detailed in Chapter 2 in this book.
9 In Wolman, *Psychoanalytic Techniques*.
10 He contrasts Ferenczi with Melanie Klein who occupied a central position in the British Psychoanalytical Society, but not with Ernest Jones, probably on account of the fact that Klein had a very global theory.
11 This criticism pervades his work, but it is to be found in particular in Balint, *The Basic Fault* and in various articles in M. Balint, *Primary Love and Psycho-Analytic Technique* (London: Karnac Books, 1994).
12 Balint, *The Basic Fault*, p. 153.
13 *Ibid.*, pp. 154–5.
14 See the two articles on Ferenczi in Balint, *Problems of Human Pleasure and Behaviour*.
15 In Balint, *Problems of Human Pleasure and Behaviour*. This text was read at a commemoration of Ferenczi in the Hungarian Psychoanalytic Society in 1933.
16 This is an allusion to an important text by Ferenczi on the early seduction of children by adults, where, among other things, he criticises the 'professional hypocrisy' of certain analysts, and where he stresses the need for 'real sincere sympathy on the

part of the analyst towards the patient when the patient is confronted with regression and intense mental trauma'. See the analysis of this text hereafter.

17 'Sandor Ferenczi' in Balint, *Problems of Human Pleasure and Behaviour*. This text was read in 1948 before the British Psychoanalytical Society on the occasion of the 15th anniversary of Ferenczi's death, and later published in the *International Journal of Psychoanalysis*.

18 This is an allusion to a text by Ferenczi where he states that too much knowledge or too much wisdom in a baby or child conceals great distress relating to experiences in infancy. See the analysis of this text hereafter.

19 See two texts on Ferenczi in Balint, *Problems of Human Pleasure and Behaviour*.

20 *Ibid.* The first object relations on which Balint did a lot of work relate to the mother–child relationship, and also to the medical sphere considered as an archaic object.

21 In Balint, *Problems of Human Pleasure and Behaviour*.

22 These articles by Ferenczi are to be found in S. Ferenczi, *First Contributions to Psycho-Analysis* (New York: Brunner/Mazel, 1980), pp. 132–53; S. Ferenczi, *Further Contributions to the Theory and the Technique of Psychoanalysis* (New York: Brunner/Mazel, 1980), pp. 311, 349, 366–78.

23 S. Freud, 'Jokes and their relation to the unconscious', *Standard Edition*, Vol. VIII (London, Hogarth Press, 1960).

24 See in particular 'The problem of language in upbringing and in psychoanalytical treatment' in Balint, *The Basic Fault*, pp. 92–8.

25 *Ibid.*, p. 160.

26 S. Ferenczi, *Final Contributions to the Problems and Methods of Psycho-Analysis* (London: Karnac Books, 1994), pp. 156–67 and 126–42. These two texts were subject to much criticism from Freud, and when Balint set out to publish the complete works of Ferenczi, Jones attempted to oppose their publication ('Correspondence Jones–Balint').

27 D. W. Winnicott, 'Ego distortion in terms of true and false self' in *The Maturational Processes and the Facilitating Environment: Studies in the Theory of Emotional Development* (London: Hogarth Press, 1965), pp. 140–52.

28 See Balint, *The Basic Fault*.

29 In Ferenczi, *Final Contributions to the Problems and Methods of Psycho-Analysis*, pp. 313–15.

30 In Ferenczi, *First Contributions to Psycho-Analysis*, pp. 193–212.

31 See M. Balint, *The Doctor, His Patient and the Illness* (London: Churchill Livingstone, 2000).

32 For Freud 'the psychical state of a sleeping person is characterized by an almost complete withdrawal from the surrounding world and a cessation of all interest in it'. S. Freud, 'A metapsychological supplement to the theory of dreams', *Standard Edition*, Vol. XIV (London: Hogarth Press, 1974), pp. 219–35.

33 Ferenczi, *Further Contributions to the Theory and the Technique of Psychoanalysis*, p. 349.

34 *Ibid.*, pp. 177–88.

35 *Ibid.*, pp. 189–98.

36 See Balint, *The Basic Fault*.

37 S. Freud, 'From the history of an infantile neurosis', *Standard Edition*, Vol. XVII (London: Hogarth Press, 1955), pp. 3–124.

38 In Ferenczi, *Further Contributions to the Theory and the Technique of Psychoanalysis*.

39 K. Obholzer, *Gespräche mit dem Wolfsmann, eine Psychoanalyse und die Folgen* (Hamburg: Verlag, 1980); *The Wolf-Man by the Wolf-Man (with The Case of the Wolf-Man by Sigmund Freud; and A Supplement)* by Ruth Mack Brunswick, foreword by Anna Freud, edited, with notes, an introduction and chapters by Muriel Gardiner (New York: Basic Books, 1981). The 'Wolf-man' died in 1977 at the age of ninety-two, after being followed by several analysts over a period of fifty years. In 1919 he returned to see Freud for several months, and Freud organised a collection because the patient could not pay for his analysis. This collection was continued for six years. When the 'wolf-man' inherited family jewels, he did not tell Freud, so that he would not discontinue the collections. Psychoanalysts continued to pay him money throughout his life, and he never paid for the sessions. Ruth M. Brunswick, his second psychoanalyst, to whom Freud addressed him, published a case report in 1929. She notes that she had to deal with 'an insufficient living-through of the transference itself' towards Freud, and that the consequence of fixing 'a time limit in analysis' was that the patient provided sufficient material to lead to his recovery and 'this resulted in the patient's bringing sufficient material to produce a cure, but it also enabled him to keep just that nucleus which later resulted in his psychosis' (in *The Wolf-Man by the Wolf-Man*, p. 304).

40 In Freud, *Standard Edition*, Vol. XVII (London: Hogarth Press, 1955), pp. 157–68.

41 In Ferenczi, *Further Contributions to the Theory and the Technique of Psychoanalysis*.

42 Budapest, along with Vienna, was one of the places of reference for psychoanalysis, and the Budapest Institute was headed by Ferenczi.

43 Written in 1921, in Ferenczi, *Further Contributions to the Theory and the Technique of Psychoanalysis*, pp. 198–216.

44 See Balint's work on brief therapies in M. Balint, P. Ornstein and E. Balint, *Focal Psychotherapy* (London: Tavistock Publications, 1972), and his desire to foster the elaboration of specific psychotherapeutic techniques for medical doctors in M. Balint, *Psychotherapeutic Techniques in Medicine* (London: Tavistock Publications, 1961).

45 See the text by S. Ferenczi, 'Introjection and transference' in *First Contributions to Psycho-Analysis*, pp. 35–93.

46 In Balint, *The Basic Fault*, pp. 99–103.

47 S. Ferenczi and O. Rank, *The Development of Psychoanalysis* (New York: Nervous and Mental Disease Publishing, 1925).

48 In Ferenczi, *Further Contributions to the Theory and the Technique of Psychoanalysis*, pp. 198–216.

49 He later revised this position, pointing, in some cases of regression, to the need to respond to the patient's needs, which explains the disagreement with Freud.

50 In Balint, *Primary Love and Psycho-Analytic Technique*, pp. 200–12.

51 In 'Sandor Ferenczi's technical experiments' in Wolman, *Psychoanalytic Techniques*.

52 See also the article by S. Ferenczi, 'On forced phantasies' in *Further Contributions to the Theory and the Technique of Psychoanalysis*, pp. 68–77.

53 In 'Sandor Ferenczi's technical experiments' in Wolman, *Psychoanalytic Techniques*.

54 Balint, *The Doctor, His Patient and the Illness*.

55 See Balint, *Primary Love and Psycho-Analytic Technique*.

56 In Ferenczi, *Further Contributions to the Theory and the Technique of Psychoanalysis*, pp. 259–96.

57 *Ibid.*, pp. 217–29.
58 'Changing therapeutical aims and techniques in psychoanalysis' and 'On the termination of analysis' in Balint, *Primary Love and Psycho-Analytic Technique*, pp. 221–35 and 236–43.
59 Ferenczi and Rank, *The Development of Psychoanalysis*.
60 Cf. Balint, *The Basic Fault* and *Primary Love and Psycho-Analytic Technique*.
61 In 'Sandor Ferenczi's technical experiments' in Wolman, *Psychoanalytic Techniques*.
62 In Ferenczi, *Final Contributions to the Problems and Methods of Psycho-Analysis*, pp. 61–76, 77–8, 87–101.
63 S. Freud, 'Analysis terminable and interminable', *Standard Edition*, Vol. XXIII (London: Karnac Books, 1975), pp. 211–53.
64 'The final goal of psycho-analytic treatment' and 'On the termination of analysis' in Balint, *Primary Love and Psycho-Analytic Technique*, pp. 188–99 and pp. 236–43.
65 In Balint, *Primary Love and Psycho-Analytic Technique*, pp. 236–43.
66 D. W. Winnicott, 'The observation of infants in a set situation' in *Through Paediatrics to Psychoanalysis* (London: Karnac Books, 1984), pp. 52–69.
67 In Balint, *The Basic Fault*, pp. 173–181.
68 'The elasticity of psycho-analytic technique' in Ferenczi, *Final Contributions to the Theory and the Technique of Psycho-Analysis*.
69 In Balint, *Primary Love and Psycho-Analytic Technique*, pp. 188–99.
70 In Ferenczi, *Final Contributions to the Problems and Methods of Psycho-Analysis*, pp. 126–42.
71 In 'The principles of relaxation and neocatharsis' in Ferenczi, *Final Contributions to the Problems and Methods of Psycho-Analysis*, pp. 108–25, he quotes a remark made to him by Anna Freud: 'You really treat your patients as I treat the children whom I analyse.'
72 See Balint, *The Basic Fault*.
73 M. Balint, *International Journal of Psychoanalysis* 50 (1969): 429–35.
74 In Ferenczi, *Final Contributions to the Problems and Methods of Psycho-Analysis*, pp. 156–67.
75 In Balint, *Primary Love and Psycho-Analytic Technique*, pp. 159–73.
76 *Ibid.*, pp. 159–73.
77 A text such as M. Balint, 'Crisis of medical practice', published in 1930 in Budapest (in *American Journal of Psychoanalysis* 62(1) (2002): 7–15), is an example from this period.
78 See S. Ferenczi, 'La psychanalyse au service de l'omnipraticien', *Psychanalyse* 3 (1982): 205–15. This is a text derived from the Conference in Kassa in 1923 on invitation from the Kassa Hungarian Physicians' Society. No English translation.
79 *Ibid.*
80 'Freud's influence on medicine' in Ferenczi, *Final Contributions to the Problems and Methods of Psycho-Analysis*, pp. 143–55.
81 S. Ferenczi, 'Présentation abrégée de la psychanalyse', *Psychanalyse* 4 (1982): 148–94. No English translation.
82 Ferenczi, 'La psychanalyse au service de l'omnipraticien', *Psychanalyse*.
83 Ferenczi, 'Présentation abrégée de la psychanalyse', *Psychanalyse*.
84 S. Ferenczi, *Thalassa: A Theory of Genitality* (New York: Psychoanalytic Quarterly, 1938), 2nd imp. Q.1933–34 (II pp. 361–403, III pp. 1–29, III pp. 200–22).
85 In Balint, *Primary Love and Psycho-Analytic Technique*, pp. 11–41.

Chapter 2

The psychoanalytic cure

Following on from Ferenczi, Balint broadened the indications of the psycho-analytic cure, taking an interest in the pre-oedipal levels of the psyche. Very early on, he questioned Freudian theory on primary narcissism, emphasising its contradictions.[1] He developed the theory of the 'primitive object-relation' and 'primary love', as well as the notion of the 'basic fault'.[2] He differentiates 'benign' regression from 'malignant' regression.[3] He describes two types of personality, the 'ocnophils' who experience a need to cling to objects, as symbols of security, and 'philobats' who are able to face up to the outside world, and attempt to control it without clinging to objects.[4]

His theories, little known today, influenced the way in which he conducted his psychoanalytic cures, the status he allocated to interpretation and transference modes, his research on psychoanalysis applied to the medical field, and the brief psychotherapies which will be the subject of subsequent chapters.

Balint's main theories

Alongside a development of psychoanalysis with children, psychotic and borderline patients, and experiments in opening up psychoanalysis to the social field following Freud's text 'Lines of advance in psychoanalytic therapy',[5] Balint widened the indications of the psychoanalytic cure, and objected to psychoanalysts who only took on neurotic patients.

The object-relation and primary narcissism

As early as 1932, he questioned the theory of primary narcissism.[6] There are, he considers, phases in the cure where 'patients expected and often demanded certain primitive gratifications [. . .] such as to be able to touch the analyst [. . .] or to be touched or stroked by him. Without exceptions, these wishes are directed towards an object and [. . .] they never go beyond the level of fore-pleasure'. Balint links these observations with very early stages in extra-uterine life, and hypothesises the existence of a 'primitive object-relation' which he contrasts with primary narcissism. He considers that it is not linked to any erogenous zone, and that its foundation is 'the instinctual interdependence of mother and child [. . .] tuned to each other', because of the physiological prematurity of the very young infant. Following up research on mother–infant interactions, which today would be referred to as ethological (Balint quotes Hermann and Alice Balint), he links the primitive object-relation to 'the tendency to cling' (the word used by Hermann) between mother and child, and to non-verbal exchanges.[7]

He considers that the aim of primary love is 'to be loved and satisfied without being under any obligation to give anything in return'. In this phase, the anaclisis provided by the other is total, and the infant does not differentiate his desires from those of his objects. He cannot conceive of them as having their own needs and desires. Balint hypothesises that primary love gives the individual 'a tranquil quiet sense of well-being'. In the 1960s,[8] he individualises a phase that precedes that of primary love, the 'phase of primary substances', during which the foetus and the infant are in harmony and interpenetration with basic elements in their undifferentiated environment (the amniotic fluid, the air). He suggests that there is a state of intense relationship with both the biological and the libidinal environment. In this phase, he considers, there is no object, 'only limitless substances or expanses'. Very frequently a breaking-off occurs too early in the primitive object-relation, or else there is an inadequate 'tuning' between mother and child, so that the individual tends to cling to an object because of a lack of internal security, frustration and insatiable desire, which are reactivated in transference.

The 'basic fault'

The 'basic fault' takes these ideas further. In 1959–60, Balint describes three levels in the psyche on the basis of the fact that certain patients are open to verbal interpretations and progress as a result of them, and are capable of a 'working-through', while others are not. The first level, the oedipal level, which is the best-mastered by analysts, is the basis of indications for the psychoanalytic cure. Whether the issue is genital or pre-genital relations, there is a triangular relationship, and this level is inseparable from psychic conflict. Adult conventional language is a sufficient and reliable means of communication (and the patient can accommodate interpretations). The second level, simpler and more primitive, he calls the 'level or area of the basic fault'. There is 'only a two-person relation', linked to the primary object-relation. Thus conflict is not the issue here. Adult language does not function. The 'basic fault' becomes central to the cure when a change in the transference situation or in the atmosphere of the session appears. The interpretations of the analyst are not perceived as such by the patient, so that the formal elements and the setting count for more than the interpretations. Patients 'feel that it is their due to receive what they need', and the analyst must find the right compromise between too great satisfaction of the patient's demands, which would risk producing 'addiction-like states', which Balint calls 'malignant regression', and excessive neutrality, which would be unbearable. Balint talks of a 'fault', a term used by his patients, because this level is linked to a lack of adjustment between the infant and the people caring for him. He defines the 'basic fault' as follows:

> The patient says that he feels there is a fault within him, a fault that must be put right. And it is felt to be a fault, not a complex, not a conflict, not a situation.[9]

The third level, even more primitive, is the 'area of creation',[10] and is, he says, characterised by the absence of any external object, which contradicts his theories of primitive object-relations: 'The subject is on his own, and his main concern is to produce something out of himself; this something to be produced may be an object, but is not necessarily so.' When the patient reaches this area, no transference occurs in the cure. What is its status? It is difficult to say. Balint talks of links with 'pre-objects' without clearly defining what they are – 'primary substances'? What are the links between this level and primary narcissism? He thinks this mode of organisation of the psyche leads to artistic creation, but also to 'two highly important phenomena: the early phases of becoming bodily- or mentally-ill, and spontaneous recovery from an illness'. Balint also hypothesises that these phenomena have a very primitive origin.

In relation to these theoretical constructions, he proposes a clinical approach to the cure organised around four main axes: the aim of the psychoanalytic treatment, the status of interpretation, the management of regression and the characteristics of transference.

The aim of the psychoanalytic treatment

As early as 1932,[11] Balint defined the finalities of the psychoanalytic cure: patients 'must learn in the course of treatment to be able again to give themselves up to love, to pleasure, to enjoyment, as fearlessly and innocently as they were able to do in their earliest childhood'. In line with Ferenczi, the issue is to retrieve the well-being that preceded the traumatic relationship with adults unable to adapt to the needs of the child. The analyst must manage the setting of the cure so that in transference the patient can experience a relation of primitive well-being, which he calls the 'new beginning'. This enables a change in the libidinal and character structure (defined as the relationship of the individual to his objects of love and hate) and in a second stage an evolution towards adult 'genital love' entailing empathy and suited to reality.[12]

The status of interpretation and the characteristics of transference

These finalities mean that the setting of cures needs to be managed so as to accommodate regression, which is not only a form of resistance, but also therapeutic. In 'The final goal of psycho-analytic treatment',[13] written in 1934, Balint describes the case of a patient he saw for a second round of treatment, and who evolved, not as a result of interpretation and working-through, which had characterised the first series of sessions, but because the analyst accommodated the regression within transference seen as an object-relation, in the here-and-now of the sessions. What mattered was not the content of the patient's associations, but formal, non-verbal elements linked to primitive object-relations, and expressing the patient's character, that is to say changes in facial expression, the way in which the patient lay down on the couch, and his manner of associating.

Thus Balint differentiates the ways in which transference occurs when the cure is on the oedipal level, and when more primitive levels emerge. The atmosphere of the cure takes on a particular form when the patient is in the area of the 'basic fault'. Words lose their power to communicate. The patient perceives interpretations as signs of hostility, or of excessive affection. He makes the analyst uneasy by becoming very perspicacious about all that concerns him, and the interpretation of his behaviours takes over the sessions. He demands naive gratifications, forcing the analyst to find the appropriate response so as to avoid either the encroachment of addiction-like states, or a break-off of the relationship. This transference, which occurs wholly within the here-and-now of the session, where only the present time of the analysis matters and where the analyst no longer appears as a person with his own needs, casts light on the archaic processes of any transference situation. This needs to be differentiated from an exacerbation of 'transference neurosis', and from 'transference-love'.[14] By differentiating benign and malignant regression and the oedipal level, it becomes possible to avoid confusing regression and an exacerbation of transference-love, and also to avoid considering manifestations such as demands to change the setting of the session, demands for gratifications, or silences solely as resistance or acting-out. This enables a modulation of the analyst's responses.

When interpretation no longer has any therapeutic value, Balint pays considerable attention to acting-out in the course of sessions, which he accepts in the same way as he accepts free associations. They are bodily enactments, creative gestures, and they favour change. Unlike hysterical symptoms, they are very close to the experience of the unconscious as it is manifested in symptoms that are bodily 'compromise formations', linked to primitive object-relations. They are not repetitions of unsatisfactory object-relations, but an experimentation, in the here-and-now of the cure and the transference, of new relationships that enable genuine upheavals in the subject's structuring. The example of a female patient somersaulting during the session illustrates this enactment of the body. Balint analyses this gesture not as a repetition, but as a childish form of behaviour and experience that enables the patient to experience a satisfactory primitive object-relation.[15] He is close to Winnicott in the attention he pays to bodily enactment in the course of sessions, even if his theorisations differ. Winnicott, in 'Withdrawal and regression' and *Holding and Interpretation: Fragment of an Analysis*, interprets the fact that a patient 'curled up and rolled over the back of the couch' in the course of a session as a bodily enactment that was 'the first direct evidence in the analysis of a spontaneous self', that is to say the expression of an authentic part of himself.[16] For Balint, in 'malignant regression', it is the satisfaction of instinctive requirements that is sought. In contrast, in 'benign regression':

> what the patient expects is not so much a gratification by an external action, but a tacit consent to use the external world in a way that would allow him to get on with his internal problems . . . being able to reach himself.[17]

The role of the analyst is to 'accept and consent to sustain and carry the patient like the earth or the water sustains and carries a man who entrusts his weight to them', and to be prepared to be used in that way. The task is to accompany the patient, offering a propping that is close to the 'holding' described by Winnicott. The theory of 'benign' and 'malignant regression' enables the analyst to differentiate between two types of act in the cure: acting-out linked to mechanisms of defence against archaic anxieties, and necessary bodily enactions showing that a new beginning is under way.

Contributions and limitations of Balint's writings on the psychoanalytic cure

Changes in relation to Freudian paradigms?

Balint's writings exhibit a breaking-away from a number of Freudian elaborations.

First of all, he belongs to the group of psychoanalysts who place the object-relation at the centre of their theorisations, with the concern to avoid restricting indications for the psychoanalytic cure to neurotics, who served as the paradigm for psychoanalysis. Like other analysts, for instance Winnicott who was his contemporary, he was concerned with developing applied psycho-analysis. However, their positions differed, despite the fact that when commenting on a talk by Winnicott[18] he places Winnicott's positions as a continuation of those expressed by Alice Balint in 1939.[19] It can also be noted in this respect that his analogies between the theory of primary love and the holding theory seem rather hasty.[20]

The hypothesis of a primitive harmony, that of primary love, spoilt or damaged by the adults in charge of the child, appears more reminiscent of Rousseau than of Freud. Balint removes the notions of 'lack' and 'psychical conflict' that belong to the subject in the Freudian model. These elements are replaced by the notion of poor 'tuning' between the child and his environment. These elaborations also contradict notions such as the 'death instinct' and masochism present in each of us.

Because he puts the emphasis on interpersonal phenomena and relations with the mother, Balint does nothing to solve the issue of the object-relation in its relation to instincts. He even clearly differentiates genital develop-ment from what he calls 'the development of object-relations'. In 'Critical notes on the theory of the pregenital organisations of the libido'[21] he writes: 'I believe that these two developments [the development of genital functions and the development of object-relations] – though frequently intertwined – are nevertheless two different processes.' And he adds in the same article:

> Intentionally, I do not inquire why oral, anal, urethral, genital etc. forms of gratification appear in the development and what they signify, but confine my problem to the question of why the attitude of the individual to his environment and especially to his love-objects changes and what are the causes of the various forms of object-relations which we describe as oral, anal, phallic, genital, narcissistic etc. love [. . .] These clinical facts are incompatible with the fundamental conceptions of the present theory of development of the libido.

The object of primary love is, according to Balint, rather a sort of lost object – a mythical satisfaction that can be retrieved, rather than a missing object that cannot be grasped. It is a real, non-fantasised, non-hallucinatory object, the mother able to prop and support the child to the full. Hatred as the first moment in a relationship with an object in the psyche is not possible, hatred follows on from the frustration at having lost the object. In 'The final goal of psychoanalytic treatment',[22] Balint describes the possibility of the development of 'a true object-relation, adjusted to reality' if the handling of regression during the cure is satisfactory.

Thus, to put it shortly, there is first an unmistakably primitive infantile object-relation, and this – if not rightly understood and treated – ends in unrealisable demands and a narcissistic state, very disagreeable for the environment [. . .] If rightly guided, however, it gives way to a relation without conflicts for the subject as well as for those around him.

Other analysts contemporary with Balint, such as Winnicott, were interested in the early relationship between mother and child, and the handling of regression. But the concept of the 'good-enough' mother (i.e. the 'ordinary devoted mother' who adapts satisfactorily to the different stages in the child's development and protects him from 'unthinkable and archaic anxieties' threatening the 'weak ego of the immature individual', and a subject 'in a state of absolute dependence') reflects the lack inherent in the subject from birth.[23] Likewise, the 'transitional object', belonging both to inner and external reality, linked to an 'intermediate area of experiencing' supposes an object that causes desire, which is inevitably missing.[24]

In his elaborations on the medical sphere, Balint links medication and 'how the doctor is prescribing himself'[25] with the primitive object-relationship, and with the 'area of the basic fault'. This, he thinks, explains the relationship of the patient with the doctor and medication, intended to help him return to this original relationship, and it also explains the difficulties in this relationship when it revives the 'basic fault'. The illness is a sort of equivalent of an archaic object, which is lacking here. Balint's conception of the object is very far removed from that of J. Lacan. Yet P. Benoit, a member of the Paris Freudian school, founded by Lacan, and trained by Balint, uses both these authors to elaborate a theory of the medical remedy as an object.[26] The illness mobilises the patient's archaic world and the 'remedy' is a transference object in the relationship with the medical sphere. The status of this object is, however, not the same as for Balint: 'It is of the order of the Real, and its presence signals an absence that the material base merely attests'. It is an illusory object, taking the place of the object that causes desire, it is linked 'to archaic objects to be found in the structure of the *id*', and it is there that the source of the non-pharmacological effects of the remedy is to be sought. Returning to the history of the complex relationship of Freud with cocaine,[27] Benoit considers that renouncing this therapeutic object, and the break that this entails, constitutes the moment of the foundation of psychoanalysis, and thus a paradigmatic element.

It seems plausible to me that the original analytic act, in the face of human distress, was, in a doctor's office, to have for the first time suspended all resort to the therapeutic object [. . .] and it was thanks to this that, once the ancestral object of the patient's transference to medicine had been removed, the analytic transference could occur, and lead to the unveiling of another object, and another again. Until at last it becomes obvious that the infinite quest for the object can only lead to its eclipse, because the quest for an object is the cause and not the end.[28]

Did Balint do away with this founding break of psychoanalysis with the therapeutic object by centring transference on the object-relation, and on the way in which the doctor (or the psychoanalyst) 'prescribes himself'? O. Mannoni[29] distinguishes the transference effect equivalent to an unprocessed form of transference, occurring in any interpersonal situation and in the therapeutic relationship, from an 'analytic' form of transference, where we can only detect the effects, and which consists in 'a displacement, a mistake as to the person'. Did Balint, when exploring the 'drug "doctor"', in fact work on an 'unprocessed' form of transference, exploring the 'sacred' dimension of the therapeutic relationship, which is also what is sought from a healer? Benoit considers that this sacred dimension makes the doctor 'a scientific healer'. It is, he thinks, related to what he calls 'the transference of God's share to humans', that is to say, 'the belief that there is somewhere, in a place to which he has no access, a knowledge of the Other embodied in clerics who for their part have free access'.

Another aspect is that the emphasis on intersubjectivity and on the authenticity of the trauma or events, apart from their actual interest value, raises a certain number of problems. Thus, linking repression solely to external influences,[30] Balint does not take into account notions such as primal repression, that is to say 'a first phase of repression which consists in the psychical (ideational) representative of the instinct being denied entrance into the conscious'.[31] This primal repression, purely intra-psychic, acts as a pole of attraction and secondarily generates 'repression proper'. Balint's conception leaves little room for the purely intra-psychic aspects of repression.

In the same way, his position in the debate concerning the reality of trauma and early trauma opens up interesting clinical perspectives, but appears as rather too linear to apprehend the many possible outcomes after trauma of this sort.

Balint's elaborations, and the weight he gives to experience and the intersubjective relation as opposed to the functioning of unconscious processes and their particular logics, thus raise the question of what A. Green called 'phenomenological empathy'[32] in psychoanalytic theory, encountered with other analysts following borderline cases and patients having experienced trauma. Is this empathy necessary, or inevitable, and does it contribute to psychoanalytic theory? The debate is open.

Balint's contributions

Balint's contributions relate mainly to transference processes, the place of language in the cure and the finalities of the analysis.

The differentiation that he introduces between psychic processes on the 'basic fault level' and castration anxiety is interesting for the conduct of cures. Unlike other analysts, when he talks of the 'gulf' on the subject of certain patients, he means above all something that is intersubjective. Winnicott[33] describes extreme 'primitive agonies' experienced by patients as a result of inappropriate early mother–infant relations, but these 'unthinkable anxieties' are first of all an original intra-psychic process linked to the immaturity of infants. In the 'Fear of breakdown',[34] primitive agonies appear when the infant is not sufficiently protected from them by maternal anaclisis. The adult patient does not have any awareness that he has already been faced with these 'primitive agonies', since 'he has not yet experienced them'. The immature ego of the infant was not able to integrate and 'encompass'[35] this experience. For Winnicott as for Balint, it is in the here-and-now of experiencing the transference that this agony can be overcome, but Winnicott's view of how it is to be overcome differs from that suggested by Balint:

> If the patient is ready for some kind of acceptance of this queer kind of truth, that what is not yet experienced did nevertheless happen in the past, then the way is open for the agony to be experienced in the transference, in reaction to the analyst's failures and mistakes. These latter can be dealt with by the patient in doses that are not excessive . . .[36]

In the cure, Balint is interested in the 'deep gulf' separating the adult analyst from the patient at the age of the 'basic fault', that is to say from the 'child in the patient',[37] or more exactly the '*infans*' ever-present in the patient. This 'deep gulf' revives primitive failures in the infant's experiences of the environment. This leads Balint to ask, in a two-person relation, how this can be overcome, and what is the role of the analyst. His reflection on the atmosphere of the analytic situation, seen as being liable to reduce the lack of tuning between patient and analyst, pervades his work, and leads him to considerations on the conduct of cures, on the status of language and on the therapeutic relationship.

Concerning the status of language in the psychoanalytic cure, Balint goes further than the mere observation that language is not efficacious for patients in a state of regression. In line with Ferenczi,[38] he states several times that for patients in a state of regression, conventional adult language, and therefore interpretation, is not intelligible. 'The presence of an adult vocabulary and an adult grammar exists only at the oedipal level' and the unconscious 'has no vocabulary in our sense; although words exist in it, they are neither more nor less than any other object representation'. They do not yet possess 'the overriding symbolic function that they will acquire in adult language'. 'They are mainly pictures, images, sounds, which may without much ado change their meaning or merge into each other – as they do, in fact, in dreams.'[39] In 'The problem of language in upbringing and in psycho-analytic treatment',[40] he describes situations where the patient finds himself obliged to learn the analyst's language, and express his affects in this language, although it is not his and he does not share it. This leads to a surface-adaptation (or a 'false self' as Winnicott puts it[41]) within the process of the psychoanalytic cure. What should be the position of the analyst when the patient is in an 'area of basic fault' or in a 'creation area'? Balint defines this in an original manner: informing and interpreting. The analyst:

> must act as interpreter between the patient's conscious adult self and his unconscious urges. In other words, it is we who have to translate for him his primitive behaviour into conventional adult language, and thus enable him to appreciate its significance.

But the analyst is also an informer, after the model of the anthropologist or the ethnologist, 'visiting a primitive tribe'. This place is occupied in a different manner by analysts working outside the field of the psychoanalytic cure (with patients in a coma, brain-damaged, autistic, demented, infants etc.). Thus with brain-damaged patients who have difficulty putting into words the unusual situation in which they find themselves, as a result of coma or cognitive disturbances, because they do not have a range of language that is shared or shareable, the analyst is often in the position of an interpreter, and needs to reduce the 'gulf' created by the experience of the illness between the patient and those with whom he needs to communicate.[42]

Further to this, if the object-relation revived in the transference is the most effective therapeutic factor when the patient is in a state of regression, how should the analyst 'prescribe himself' in order 'to create the object-relationship which, in Balint's opinion, is the most suitable for that particular patient'?[43] In certain periods in the psychoanalytic cure, the use of interpretation merely reinforces the inequality of the relation between patient and analyst. The analyst, in all events, is liable to appear as 'omnipotent' to the patient, exacerbating his dependence. By being 'a provider of time and milieu', and allowing the patient to relate to him as if he were a 'primary substance',[44] the analyst helps the patient to 'discover his way to the world of objects'.[45] Balint is close to Winnicott's conceptions of the analytic process as he describes it in 'The observation of infants in a set situation'.[46] Indeed, Winnicott quotes *The Basic Fault* when talking of the reliability of the therapeutic setting that the analyst should offer the patient in a state of regression, and the fact that he should sometimes allow for sequences of unconnected thought:

> Perhaps it is to be accepted that there are patients who at times need the therapist to note the nonsense that belongs to the mental state of the individual at rest without the need even for the patient to communicate

this nonsense, that is to say, without the need for the patient to organize nonsense. Organized nonsense is already a defence, just as organized chaos is a denial of chaos.[47]

However, Balint puts more emphasis on the structural inequality of the relationship between analyst and patient, and on the bodily restraint required by the cure (lying down, not getting up from the couch). This is 'a kind of holding the patient tight', and analogous with the gesture of an adult taking a child into his arms to calm him down.[48] In reference to the practical management of the cure, Balint talks of 'restraint by symbolic action on the part of the analyst'. The cure, classically centred on language and the suspension of the act, is also an act of symbolic bodily constraint.

The same concern with understanding the way in which the therapist prescribes himself, and with creating conditions enabling doctor and patient to be 'tuned in'[49] can be found in several concepts developed by Balint relating to medical practice. In *The Doctor, His Patient and the Illness*, he focuses on 'the patient's offers' and 'the doctor's responses', and on the notion of the 'drug "doctor"'. The way in which the doctor responds to the symptoms and the discourse of the patient, and his ability to create a 'Mutual Investment Company' between doctor and patient on the basis of sometimes long-standing, intimate links, are very important in the doctor–patient relationship, and in the functioning of the Balint groups. Towards the end of his life, Balint worked on the 'flash technique', that is to say on the means available to the doctor in the course of short consultations to produce 'brief, intense, intimate contacts between doctor and patient', 'a peculiar intense flash of understanding between the doctor and the patient',[50] which alters the way in which the patient sees himself and his symptoms.

Balint's conceptions of the finalities of analysis are above all therapeutic, and relate to reparation, even if he modulates his position in his last writings. In 'Character analysis and new beginning',[51] he considers the analysis should repair a traumatic breakdown in the primary love relation, and enable it to be restored with an idealisation of the supposed well-being that it brings. It needs to be re-conquered by way of the transference relationship so as to move on from the effects of an original trauma. Thus re-conquering, rather than any form of interpretation, is what enables a significant change in the psychic structure of the patient and his relationship with himself and others, that is to say his 'character'.[52] The patient 'still has to learn anew to be able to love innocently, unconditionally, as only children can love'. A new definition of 'working through' appears:

This last stage in the analytic treatment, the working through of the resistances, or as I should like to call it: *the search after a new beginning free from anxiety*, always brings with it an extension of the capacity of love and enjoyment. (Original emphasis)

The 'new beginning' in the course of the cure enables the finalities of the analysis to be reached, the adaptive aims of which are clear: 'the capacity to enjoy full genital satisfaction, i.e. mature genitality', and a strong enough ego 'which enables the individual to maintain an uninterrupted contact with reality even under strain'.[53]

This is a long way from the elaborations on the 'analytic act'.[54] Here the conduct of the cure is more focused on the imaginary than on the symbolic. Lacan, in 'The function and field of speech and language in psychoanalysis',[55] defines Balint's practice and theory as follows:

Analysis is becoming a relation of two bodies between which is established a phantasmatic communication in which the analyst teaches the subject to apprehend himself as an object; subjectivity is admitted into it only within the parentheses of the illusion, and speech is placed on the index of a search for the lived experience that becomes its supreme aim.

It is also far removed from the structural '*méconnaissance*' (not translated in the English editions of Lacan's work) of the subject, never overcome.

Balint's positions concerning the finalities of the analysis were to evolve. As early as 1949 he noted that analysts have little scope for evaluating the effects of cures after the fact, and that in his practice, which was restricted, he only observed an ideal terminal phase in two cases out on ten.[56] In 'The hazards inherent in managing the regression',[57] he criticises the notion of limitless giving by the analyst, which he attributes to Ferenczi. This technique for managing regression could allow 'addiction-like states in the psycho-analytic cure'. Creating the conditions for the disappearance of all suffering is a myth. When the analyst manages regression by too readily meeting the needs of the patient, both patient and analyst are liable to undergo the counter-transference of the analyst seeking to do good without limitation. This can generate hatred in the transference and counter-transference,[58] the counterpart of which is an attempt at greater sincerity by the analyst, leading to pointless justifications, mishandling and inadequacy.[59]

In 'Bridging the gulf',[60] Balint defines a process of grieving for the loss of the original object of love, and the presence of a 'scar' or a 'fault' in the psychic structure that the patient must accept. Thus the complaints of the patient must be accepted without interpretation, leaving him time to convert his resentment into regret. In a footnote, he criticises his earlier positions concerning the finalities of the analysis and the idealised image that he entertained. He very subtly attributes this to 'an over-compensation of the basic fault', also found in the patient. Renouncing it is part of the mourning process in the cure, which the analyst should discreetly accompany. He defines his position as that of a 'witness', again an original position. Other analysts caring for patients with serious trauma have also talked of the role of witness occupied by the analyst[61] to help them get through and overcome a traumatic experience. Thus Daniel, a child receiving treatment for cancer, wanted above all to hand on his experience, via the therapeutic process, and wanted the analyst to witness this. This is why he says to the analyst: 'Do not throw my drawings in the bin', which led to a book on this psychotherapy, which lasted three years and terminated with the death of the child.[62]

Following this overview of the psychoanalytic cure, Balint appears as a clinician who mistrusts theoretical claims that are too readily generalised. The wealth of his writings is above all linked to his cautiousness towards ready-made recipes, his concern to explore new fields, his clinical practice and the numerous comments throughout his work. The impact of his work mainly derives from the importance he attaches to the object-relation and intersubjectivity, which, despite their limitations, are notions that have the merit of opening up analysis to new perspectives. By seeking to understand the theoretical foundations of 'two-person psychology', Balint enriched psychoanalytic theory by using material from outside that field. Other psychoanalysts, like Lacan, Winnicott and Bion, have done the same with different theorisations and methods. All this has enriched psychoanalytic theory and opened the way for the development of applied psychoanalysis.

Notes

1 M. Balint, 'Early developmental states of the ego: Primary object-love' in *Primary Love and Psycho-Analytic Technique* (London: Karnac Books, 1994), pp. 90–108, text of a lecture in Budapest in 1937 and later published in *Imago* 23 (1937): 270–88 and in the *International Journal of Psychoanalysis* 30 (1949): 265–73; 'Character analysis and new beginning' in the same work, pp. 159–73, text presented in Wiesbaden in 1932; 'Primary narcissism and primary love', *Psychoanalytic Quarterly* 29(1) (1960): 6–43, returned to in M. Balint, *The Basic Fault* (Evanston, IL: Northwestern University Press, 1992).

2 Balint, *The Basic Fault* returns to two articles written in the 1960s and develops them: 'The regressed patient and his analyst,' *Psychiatry* XXIII (1960): 231–43; 'The three areas of mind', presented in the USA in 1956–7.

3 See Balint, *The Basic Fault*, in particular, 'The benign and the malignant forms of regression', pp. 119–58.

4 M. Balint, *Thrills and Regression* (London: Hogarth, 1959). We will not dwell on these aspects in this chapter.

5 In S. Freud, 'Lines of advance in psychoanalytic therapy', *Standard Edition*, Vol. XVII (London: Hogarth Press, 1955), pp. 157–68.

6 See note 1 and 'The final goal of psychoanalytic treatment' in Balint, *Primary Love and Psycho-Analytic Technique*, pp. 188–99, a text first presented in 1934 at the 13th International Psychoanalysis Conference.

7 'Critical notes on the theory of pregenital organisations of the libido' in Balint, *Primary Love and Psycho-Analytic Technique*, pp. 49–72.

8 See Balint, *The Basic Fault* and *Thrills and Regression*.

9 Balint, *The Basic Fault*, and in particular 'The two levels of analytic work', pp. 11–17 and 'The area of the basic fault', pp. 18–23.

10 'The area of creation' in Balint, *The Basic Fault*, pp. 24–7. Balint also mentions this in *The Doctor, His Patient and the Illness* (London: Churchill Livingstone, 2000).

11 See 'Character analysis and new beginning' in Balint, *Primary Love and Psycho-Analytic Technique*, pp. 159–73. This text was published before Ferenczi died in 1933.

12 See also 'On the termination of analysis' in Balint, *Primary Love and Psycho-Analytic Technique,* pp. 236–43.

13 In Balint, *Primary Love and Psycho-Analytic Technique*, pp. 188–99.

14 'Regression and the child in the patient' in Balint, *The Basic Fault*, pp. 79–91.

15 'Symptomatology and diagnosis' in Balint, *The Basic Fault*, pp. 127–32.

16 D. W. Winnicott, 'Withdrawal and regression' in *Through Paediatrics to Psycho-analysis* (London: Karnac Books, 1984), pp. 255–61 and D. W. Winnicott, *Holding and Interpretation: Fragment of an Analysis* (London: Karnac Books, 1986).

17 'The various forms of therapeutic regression' in Balint, *The Basic Fault*, pp. 138–48.

18 Intervention on reports by D. W. Winnicott and P. Greenacre, International Psycho-analysis Conference, Edinburgh, 30 July–3 August 1961.

19 See the article by Alice Balint, 'Love for the mother and mother love' in Balint, *Primary Love and Psycho-Analytic Technique*, pp. 109–27.

20 Balint worked on occasion with Winnicott on the question of the 'flash' technique (see hereafter), and his second wife was analysed by him (see M. Moreau-Ricaud, *Michael Balint: Le renouveau de l'école de Budapest* (Ramonville Sainte-Agne: Erès, 2000)).

21 In Balint, *Primary Love and Psycho-Analytic Technique*, pp. 49–72, text of a lecture in 1935.

22 In Balint, *Primary Love and Psycho-Analytic Technique,* pp. 188–99.

23 D. W. Winnicott, 'Mind and its relation to the psyche-soma' in *Through Paediatrics to Psychoanalysis*, pp. 243–54.

24 D. W. Winnicott, 'Transitional objects and transitional phenomena' in *Playing and Reality* (London: Routledge, 1989), pp. 1–25.

25 See Balint, *The Doctor, His Patient and the Illness*.

26 P. Benoit, *Chroniques médicales d'un psychanalyste* (Paris: Rivages, 1988); P. Benoit, 'Inconscient et thérapeutique médicamenteuse', *Le Coq Héron* 66 (1978).

27 See also S. Freud, *De la cocaïne* (Brussels: Editions Complexes, 1976).

28 Benoit, *Chroniques médicales d'un psychanalyste*.

29 O. Mannoni, 'La férule' in *Ça n'empêche pas d'exister* (Paris: Le Seuil, 1982), pp. 63–84.

30 In 'The final goal of psycho-analytic treatment' in *Primary Love and Psycho-Analytic Technique*, Balint writes: 'One thing we should never forget is that all these defects of development, which we group under the collective name of "the

repressed", were originally forced into that state by external influences. . . . There is no repression without reality, without an object-relation.'

31 S. Freud, 'Repression', *Standard Edition*, Vol. XIV (London: Hogarth Press, 1957), pp. 142–58.
32 A. Green, *La folie privée* (Paris: Gallimard, 1990).
33 D. W. Winnicott, 'Fear of breakdown' in *Psycho-Analytic Explorations* (London: Karnac Books, 1989), pp. 87–95.
34 *Ibid.*
35 The word used by Winnicott.
36 In 'Fear of breakdown' in Winnicott, *Psycho-Analytic Explorations*.
37 This phrase was used by Ferenczi.
38 See Chapter 1 in this book.
39 'The problem of language in upbringing and in psycho-analytic treatment' in Balint, *The Basic Fault*, pp. 92–7.
40 *Ibid.*
41 D. W. Winnicott, 'The concept of the false self' in *Home Is Where We Start from* (London: Penguin Books, 1990), pp. 65–70.
42 H. Oppenheim-Gluckman, *La pensée naufragée* (Paris: Anthropos, 2014) for the 3rd edition.
43 'Therapeutic regression, primary love, and the basic fault' and 'The unobtrusive analyst', in Balint, *The Basic Fault*, pp. 159–72 and pp. 173–81.
44 *Ibid.*
45 'The unobtrusive analyst' in Balint, *The Basic Fault*, pp. 173–81.
46 In Winnicott, *Through Paediatrics to Psychoanalysis*, pp. 52–69. See Chapter 1 of this book.
47 D. W. Winnicott, 'Playing: Creative activity and the search for the self' in *Playing and Reality*, pp. 53–64.
48 'Bridging the gulf' in Balint, *The Basic Fault*, pp. 182–88.
49 E. Balint and J. S. Norell, *Six Minutes for the Patient* (London: Tavistock Publications, 1973). This book describes the last research work by Balint and his colleagues. It was published after his death.
50 M. Balint, 'Research in psychotherapy' in Balint and Norell, *Six Minutes for the Patient*, pp. 1–18. Research on the flash technique has points in common with Winnicott's work, and Balint mentions that he invited Winnicott to take part in his research.
51 In Balint, *Primary Love and Psycho-Analytic Technique*, pp. 159–73.
52 'Character analysis and new beginning' in Balint, *Primary Love and Psycho-Analytic Technique*, pp. 159–73.
53 'On the termination of analysis' in Balint, *Primary Love and Psycho-Analytic Technique*, pp. 236–43.
54 J. Lacan, 'The function and field of speech and language in psychoanalysis' in *Ecrits: A Selection* (London: Routledge, 2001), pp. 33–125.
55 *Ibid.*
56 'On the termination of analysis' in Balint, *Primary Love and Psycho-Analytic Technique*, pp. 236–43.
57 In Balint, *The Basic Fault*, pp. 110–18.
58 Here Balint is referring to Winnicott's article 'Hate in the countertransference' in *Through Paediatrics to Psychoanalysis*, pp. 194–203, but his elaboration is very different from that by Winnicott. For Winnicott, there is a latent hatred of the analyst in any analytic process. In ordinary analysis, the analyst does not have

difficulty managing it. But certain patients arouse his hatred, which then takes over the transference process. Winnicott hypothesises that 'the mother hates the baby before the baby hates the mother and before the baby can know his mother hates him', and that 'the analyst must find himself in a position comparable to that of the mother of a new-born baby'.

59 This is an implicit criticism of Ferenczi, who stressed the importance of sincerity in the analyst, and denounced the risk of hypocrisy in the transference relationship.

60 In Balint, *The Basic Fault*, pp. 182–8.

61 Although it takes on different forms from that described by Balint.

62 D. Oppenheim, *Ne jette pas mes dessins à la poubelle* (Paris: Le Seuil, 1999).

Chapter 3

The training of psychoanalysts

Balint wrote only two articles on the training of psychoanalysts. These articles, which are polemic in style, denounce what he calls the 'inhibited thinking' abounding in psychoanalytic societies.[1] Written in 1947 and 1953, they should be seen in the context of the debates underway in these societies. One is the text of a lecture delivered to the British Psychoanalytical Society in 1947, and the other is a talk to the London Psychoanalysis Conference in July 1953. In the first article, Balint takes issue with the new ruling of the English school, in stating a distinction between the analyst undertaking a training analysis and the analyst who supervises the cases of the candidate analyst, which went against the proposals of Ferenczi and the Budapest Institutes. This text is a follow-up to his earlier criticisms of the training system in the English school.[2] The year 1953 saw the split in the Paris Psychoanalysis Society in France, and the creation of the French Psychoanalysis Society (Société Française de Psychanalyse). One the issues in this split was the question of the training of psychoanalysts and the place of training analysis. Balint's second article is mostly focused on this theme. In the London Conference in July 1953, a committee made up of Winnicott, Lampl de Groot, Greenacre, Eisler and Hoofer was to reach a decision on the application by the Société Française de Psychanalyse to become affiliated with the International Psychoanalytic Association (IPA), and on the question of training analysis. Balint proposed a reconciliation process, and the appointment of the split fraction members as IPA members on an individual basis.[3] Beyond these contextual aspects, these articles were written for the purpose of defending the achievements of the Budapest Institutes, in a period during which Balint was involved in wider reflection on the diffusion of psychoanalysis outside the psychoanalytic environment. He wanted to develop a form of psychotherapy 'for the masses',[4] as shows clearly in his work with groups of general practitioners, and his concern with developing specific training courses and a psychotherapy suited to their practice, grounded in psychoanalysis.[5]

The question of pedagogy

The question of pedagogy in the cure was present at a very early stage in Balint's work. In 1938, following the debate between Freud and Ferenczi,[6] Balint wrote an article entitled 'Strength of the ego and ego-pedagogy',[7] in which he wonders about 'what the significance and the function of pedagogy within the analytical treatment actually is'. Without explicitly quoting Freud's text 'Lines of advance in psychoanalytic therapy',[8] and without actually distancing himself from certain texts by Ferenczi, he notes that thus far pedagogy has above all concerned the strengthening of the super-ego. Since he is not only dealing with neurotic patients, but also 'borderline' cases, he considers that there is a need to develop 'an education to analysis' simultaneously with the cure, addressed to the ego, that is to say an 'Ego-pedagogy or education of the Ego'. This is not the 'introjection of commands', which fosters passivity and the development of the super-ego, but 'becoming experienced to enrich and develop the Ego', which he describes above all as corporeal. This position shows his concern to differentiate knowledge, or interpretations that are artificially superimposed so that the subject can only access them in the super-ego mode, from training or pedagogy by way of the acquiring of experiences that the subject can feel and appropriate. This has repercussions, first of all on the way in which cures are conducted – the analyst needs to exercise discretion while the patient makes his own discoveries at his own pace[9] – and, second, on the training systems implemented with doctors.

The 'dead-ends' in the training of psychoanalysts and their consequences

Balint's articles on the training of psychoanalysts return to the same concerns. What is interesting in his positions is the criticism of the way in which psychoanalysis is handed on, generating dogmatic analytic institutions with members who are alienated from the master's discourse, something Balint always refused. In the light of the history of the psychoanalytic movement, including the present-day situation, Balint's analysis is very interesting, and can still provide material for reflection on the transmission of psychoanalysis in psychoanalytic institutions, and on their functioning. It is a healthy reminder of the ever-present risks.

The risk of totalitarianism

Recalling the proposals of the Budapest Institute – according to which therapeutic analysis cannot be separated from training analysis, and the two, along with control analysis, should be conducted by one and the same analyst, at least for the candidate's first case – Balint severely criticises the functioning of the psychoanalytic institutions and the modes of transmission of psycho-analytic practice. The problem of training, he says, has been little broached over the last twenty-five years in psychoanalytical institutions, and this is very damaging. He describes two trends in these institutions: 'inhibited thinking' and a 'tendency to be dogmatic'. Candidates are alienated from the training analysts, which hampers the analytic process, which then becomes 'a primitive initiation ceremony [. . .] which forces the candidate to identify himself with his initiator, to introject the initiator and his ideals, and to build up from these identifications a strong superego'. This goes against freedom of thought and action with oneself, to which psychoanalysis should lead. This type of training generates processes of alienation and strengthens the super-ego instead of developing an ego-pedagogy, and it also generates a religious-type relationship, without critical analysis, towards the psycho-analytic institutions. This religious relationship, rarely avoided by the psychoanalytic institutions, with its counterpart of totalitarianism, is a threat to all institutions, as can be seen from the events of the twentieth century.

Although Balint was writing his texts after the Second World War, in the heyday of Stalinism, he does not indulge in any such generalisations. Nor does he make any reference to the group theory or institutions while working in the Tavistock Clinic with Bion.[10] He does not mention Freud's text 'Group psychology and the analysis of the ego',[11] which describes the crowd as 'a revival of the primal horde'. According to Freud, the individuals making it up put the leader (or 'head') 'in the place of the ego ideal' and act under the illusion 'of there being a head who loves all the individuals in the group with an equal love'. On several occasions Balint uses the word 'conversion' to characterise the changes in the theoretical positions of members of analytic institutions, seemingly with the meaning of the 'conversion' of Saint Paul. He links these 'conversions' to the super-ego type training in psychoanalytic institutions, but also to the conversion of Saint Paul who teaches us 'that introjecting a previously hated and persecuted object in idealized form may result in intolerance, sectarianism, and apostolic fury'. Quite apart from its relevance in relation to the psychoanalytic institutions, Balint's remark is probably also linked to his personal history. Balint, whose father was a doctor of Jewish origin, according to M. Moreau-Ricaud[12] changed his family name and converted to Unitarianism in the 1920s. He appears to have had a complex relationship with his father. Balint emigrated to London to escape from Nazism. His family remained in Hungary and his sister was strongly attached to her Jewish identity. Both his parents committed suicide in 1944 to escape from Nazism. His sister, brother-in-law and nephew survived the Holocaust despite being deported to Bergen-Belsen. Balint always remained discreet on the subject of his private life. When he alludes to conversions in the psychoanalytic movement, is he returning to his own conversion, and does he feel the need to differentiate himself from Saint Paul? The text of 1953 ends with the motto of the Unitarian Church: 'Reform unremittingly', but it also concludes with reflection on the question of hate, somewhat out of line with his theory of primary love.

Training analysis and transference

Balint refers to two partial but important elements to explore the characteristics of transference in training analysis. First, his historical analysis of the psychoanalytic movement raises – but does not answer – a question that is still relevant today: how does an institution, or a discipline, manage the inheritance of its founder with its limitations? Second, he wonders how far the organisation of training analysis and control analysis might generate specific transference problems. He does not view the transference situation as an intrinsic component of the risk of alienation, although he does consider questions such as the risk of 'malignant regression' which generates very strong dependence and submission towards the analyst and difficulty in reducing transference.[13] He quotes Freud's text 'Analysis terminable and interminable', where Freud argues with Ferenczi on two points, the active technique and the illusion of an analysis that might be fully complete, but not on the central theme of the text, which is that intrinsically any analysis comes up against the 'underlying bedrock' linked to the 'biological'.[14] He does, however, show interest in Freud's remarks on training analysis: it does not enable the mental health norm established for patients to be reached. The solution proposed by Freud for analysis every five years is not, according to Balint, actually implemented, and he subscribes to his scepticism on Ferenczi's idea of a 'fully completed analysis'[15] for analysts. This position, like his concluding remark in the 1953 article concerning something that is non-analysable, linked to hate, seems to partially contradict his theories of the 'New beginning' and 'Primary love' without psychic conflict.[16]

One of the consequences of both the myth of a fully completed analysis and the limitations of training analysis is the development of 'post-training analyses', which evidences the contradictions and the limits of the training system. Balint very aptly wonders if these analyses enable the future analyst to genuinely undertake an analytic process, given that his privacy is protected and career issues no longer intervene in the analytic process. These 'post-training analyses' show the inefficiency of the training system and the rules of training analysis, or could even support the myth of a normality that can be reached by way of a 'super-therapy'.[17]

Balint's remarks on the transference effects of training analysis and control analysis are still valid today, although his proposals were restricted. The analyst is introjected in any analytic process, but it is an unreal image that can be subjected to a working-through in the setting of the reduction of the transference. The separation between patient and analyst enables the place of this introjection to be contained, but this is not so in training analyses where the analysand and the analyst belong to the same institution. In this case, and in particular at the time of control analysis, the introjected analyst possesses too much reality. The required neutrality can no longer be observed, so that the candidate has no psychic freedom, there is difficulty reducing transference, and the training analyst inevitably occupies an all-powerful position. The candidate very often makes allowances for his analyst, and cannot presume to allow transference in which there is hatred or hostility, this being all the more true because it is liable to be too systematically interpreted. In case of conflict within the institution, which the candidate will know of, the analyst can appear endangered and the candidate absorbed in a fantasy of saving him as if he were a parent figure. It is more difficult for the candidate to relinquish the introjected ideals of the analyst when this analyst is under criticism, and when the candidate's attitude is liable to be assimilated to agreeing with the criticism, and hence to a sort of betrayal.

The 'bedrock' of hatred

Despite the severity of these observations, Balint's proposals are not far-reaching, and they do not provide answers to the structural issues raised by the training of analysts. Freud's text 'Lines of advance in psychoanalytic therapy'[18] broaches the question of the mingling of educational and analytic influences in the cure,[19] and secondarily recommends caution in the use of an educative attitude in the cure, so that the patient does not take it solely as a super-ego and identification element and so that the analyst respects his freedom. Balint quotes this text to encourage training analysts to exercise the same caution. But he does not say how the pitfalls of the analytic situation, in particular the didactic pitfalls, can be avoided. As in other texts, he proposes avoiding over-systematic interpretation, in particular regarding hate and hostility, in the transference. He strongly recommends more flexibility and less dogmatism in debates. The end of his second article possibly casts light on the limitations of his elaboration. Curiously, he concludes on the fact that the analysis, and of course training analysis, comes up against the 'bedrock' of hatred: 'As we all know, dealing with aggressive impulses, with hatred, has always been one of the unsolved, and perhaps insoluble, problems of mankind, causing troubles far beyond the field of psycho-analytical training.' Here, Balint seems at odds with the rest of his work. Yet, it is on this reflection that he concludes the book *Primary Love and Psycho-Analytic Technique*, in the first edition of which this article forms the final chapter.

Notes

1 M. Balint, 'On the psycho-analytic training system', *International Journal of Psychoanalysis* (1948), 29 and 'Analytic training and training analysis', *International Journal of Psychoanalysis* (1954), 35. These two articles were published in the first edition (1965) of *Primary Love and Psycho-Analytic Technique* (London: Tavistock Publications), pp. 253–85, but were not included in the subsequent versions.

2 See M. Moreau-Ricaud: *Michael Balint: le renouveau de l'école de Budapest* (Ramonville Saint-Agne: Erès, 2000).

3 E. Roudinesco, *La bataille de cent ans*, Vol. II (Paris: Le Seuil, 1986).

4 Balint, 'On the psycho-analytic training system', *International Journal of Psychoanalysis*.

5 M. Balint, *The Doctor, His Patient and the Illness* (London: Churchill Livingstone, 2000) was published in 1957, and the Balint groups started up in the 1950s.

6 See Chapter 1 in this book.

7 In Balint, *Primary Love and Psycho-Analytic Technique*, pp. 200–12.

8 In S. Freud, 'Lines of advance in psychoanalytic therapy', *Standard Edition*, Vol. XVII (London: Hogarth Press, 1955), pp. 157–68.

9 See M. Balint, *The Basic Fault* (Evanston, IL: Northwestern University Press, 1992).

10 The absence of any explicit theoretical reference to the group theory is also true for Balint groups. Yet Balint wanted psychoanalytic theory to become 'Two-Body, Three-Body, Four-Body and Multi-Body Psychology' and wanted it to be enriched by group psychotherapy and the study of 'natural' groups (neighbours' communities, works groups etc.). See, for instance, 'Changing therapeutical aims and techniques in psycho-analysis' in Balint, *Primary Love and Psycho-Analytic Technique*, pp. 221–35.

11 In S. Freud, 'Group psychology and the analysis of the ego', *Standard Edition*, Vol. XVIII (London: Hogarth Press, 1955), pp. 66–143.

12 For further details see also what Balint's son had to say, in Moreau-Ricaud, *Michael Balint: le renouveau de l'école de Budapest*, pp. 235–41.

13 See Chapter 2 in this book.

14 S. Freud, 'Analysis terminable and interminable', *Standard Edition*, Vol. XXIII (London: Hogarth Press, 1964), pp. 211–53.

15 S. Ferenczi, 'The problem of the termination of the analysis' in *Final Contributions to the Problems and Methods of Psycho-Analysis* (London: Karnac Books, 1994), pp. 77–86.

16 He also criticised this theory later in *The Basic Fault*.

17 According to Balint these 'post-training' analyses were conducted with the same analyst.

18 In Freud, 'Lines of advance in psychoanalytic therapy', *Standard Edition*, Vol. XVII, pp. 157–68.

19 See Chapter 1 in this book.

Part II

Applied psychoanalysis

Chapter 4

The issue of psychotherapies

Balint's work on brief forms of psychotherapy is still relevant to the ongoing debate today on the subject of the status of psychotherapies. Although this work is little known, Balint took an interest very early in what he described as 'psychotherapy for a larger segment of the population'. At the time of the very first training groups for doctors set up in England he set out to develop a specific form of psychotherapy for use by general practitioners, based on the knowledge acquired in psychoanalysis but without artificially imitating it.[1] He also defined the terms of psychotherapies to be conducted by non-analysts other than doctors, in particular social workers. Alongside the 'focal therapy workshop', he formalised the practice of 'brief' psychotherapies, to be conducted by psychoanalysts.

Historical aspects

Psychotherapeutic Techniques in Medicine[2] was published in 1961. The book originated from research and training seminars for doctors organised by Balint in 1949 in the Tavistock Clinic.[3] It also gives consideration to wider issues concerning the practice of psychotherapy by non-analysts, and draws on Balint's experience with social workers, psychologists and psychiatrists. His writings on the 'flash' technique, which aimed to define the conditions for a psychotherapeutic relationship in the setting of a normal consultation in general medicine, lasting six minutes on average, resulted from research work over a period of five years from 1966 to 1971.[4]

Research on the brief psychotherapies practised by psychoanalysts ran parallel to that on brief psychotherapies conducted by doctors. A group of analysts from the Tavistock Clinic in London and Cassel Hospital in Richmond, known as the 'Focal Therapy Workshop' and supervised by Balint, formed between 1955 and 1961. This led to a book entitled *A Study of Brief Psychotherapy* by Malan,[5] describing research conducted from 1955 and 1958. Malan is considered to be one of the founders of brief psychotherapies.

However, he clearly states in this book that his work developed on the initiative of Balint and under his supervision. The research group was disbanded in 1961. Balint's book entitled *Focal Therapy*[6] was completed in 1971, after his death. It describes a brief psychotherapy that lasted fifteen months with sessions at variable intervals, and a follow-up lasting six and a half years. There were episodic contacts with the patient after the end of this psychotherapy, and then over two and a half years with the patient's doctor.

Methods

The focal therapy workshop

The way this was run inevitably raises questions for the analytic community today, at a time when one of the issues in hand is the evaluation of psychotherapies, and when part of the psychoanalytic movement, in particular in the USA, has produced scientific data on psychoanalytic cures or psychotherapies and their effects[7] that are, however, contested by other analysts. The focal therapy workshop was at once a 'research-action' group[8] that used methods of 'scientific' research, a group in charge of the supervision of clinical cases with reference to psychoanalysis, and a training and inter-training group. Its aim was to develop a systematic brief form of psychotherapy that could be defined, taught, improved and evaluated for its effects. This brief psychotherapy was not, according to Balint and the participants in the research group, a contradiction with regard to the psychoanalytical approach, since brief or focal psychotherapy was in fact an extension of psychoanalysis. The group opposed those who thought that there was a watertight boundary between psychoanalysis and psychotherapy. To develop this approach, they considered that analysts 'would have to take some risks',[9] and certain changes would be required to the classic techniques of psychoanalysis.

Since the work on brief psychotherapies was research, the group developed a research methodology that was compatible with methods prevailing in the 1960s in the areas of psychology and psychiatry, for several reasons. First, Balint wanted to widen the applications of psychoanalysis and to address not only analysts, but also the scientific community, doctors and social workers, and to publish his work outside the psychoanalytical sphere. For instance, he published several articles on Balint groups and the training of doctors in medical psychology in *The Lancet*, one of the top medical journals. Second, he had a focus on accuracy and thoroughness, aiming to gain a better understanding of the long-term effects of analytical and psychotherapeutic work, and the processes of change this could operate. The group conducted bibliographic searches on the therapeutic results of cures published by psychoanalytical research, and noted that because of a failure to ensure follow-up, in most of the published work, it was not known whether the improvements described were linked to transference effects or were lasting. These inconsistencies in reporting and assessing the effects of the cures compromised the validity of the psychoanalytical method within the scientific community and also more generally outside the psychoanalytical sphere. Balint was always conscious of the need for follow-up of cases, a recurrent theme in the research and doctor training seminars that he organised, as it was in his research work and in his own case reports. Finally, Balint, because of his scientific and medical training – he obtained a science doctorate in Berlin in the 1920s and an MSc in 1945 with a thesis on research into genetic psychology[10] – was acquainted with research methods and he made use of them where he thought fit, in very eclectic manner and very freely, with no preconceived ideas as to what would suit the analysis. However, his focus on research methods viewed as 'scientific' in the 1960s and 1970s and his determination to publish in scientific journals led him in some cases to publish results in the form of percentages, which can appear ill-suited, rather naive and not very useful in relation to the wealth of clinical material in his writings, and the questions he raised. Likewise, in *Six Minutes for the Patient* we find the precursors of the evaluation scales, widely criticised today, designed to allocate scores to the patient's symptoms, to tensions in the patient's close circle and to therapeutic achievements. This probably reflected an over-ambitious emphasis on scientific validity.

Malan, supervised by Balint, evaluated the short- and long-term results of brief psychotherapies, first from twenty-one cases (the subject of his book) and at a later stage from some fifty cases. In *Focal Psychotherapy*, Balint, considering that Malan's work made it possible to assess the therapeutic results of brief psychotherapies, decided to use the in-depth study of one case to explore the psychotherapeutic process, or what he termed 'the interaction between the patient's associations and the therapist's choice of interventions'.[11]

The 'Focal Therapy Workshop' met once a week for two-hour discussions on different cases. The twenty-one cases reported by Malan involved seven therapists. Balint himself, despite his particular status, reported on his work. A case analysis grid or form served to standardise the research data. In relation to the present-day debate on the relationships between psychotherapy and psychoanalysis, it is interesting to note that these forms, the layout of which evolved, originated from the forms used for work on marital difficulties with social workers in the Family Discussion Bureau.[12] A projective test was performed for each patient included in the research before and after psychotherapy treatment, and the patient was seen in follow-up, or else contacts were established either with the patient himself or with the person who referred him, so as to assess the effects of treatment in the long term. In the cases cited by Balint, follow-up after treatment lasted six and a half years, and in those quoted by Malan they lasted up to five years.

In the cases quoted by Balint, the forms used differed from those used by Malan. They had been altered on account of Balint's research objectives: 'to study object-relationships not merely in terms of fantasies about and reconstructions of the past, but object-relationships that could be observed in the current life of the patient and in the interview situation'.[13] Balint sought in this way to formalise the 'atmosphere' or 'setting'[14] of the session, and to focus on the 'here-and-now'. After the encounter, he wrote a report on each session, which he dictated to a secretary, endeavouring to respond in a circumstantial and descriptive manner to a set of questions. For instance, in the first interview he noted how the patient was referred, the patient's appearance and manner, his complaints, what appeared to have brought him there at that time, the patient's conception of himself and of other people, the doctor–patient relationship, how the doctor treated the patient and how the patient treated the doctor, the salient features of the interview, the ways in which the disturbance showed up in the patient's life, the interpretation of all the above in dynamic terms, the suitability for focal therapy and points against it. Thus in *Focal Psychotherapy* he very precisely describes telephone and postal contacts with the correspondents who addressed Mr Baker to him, and their atmosphere, the patient's attitude, his manner of dress, the way he told his story, his earlier and present complaints, and the family history as told by the patient. The idea that the patient had of himself is summed up in a few lines: 'a reliable, sensible, very loving man . . . Very troubled by his worries and he feels he needs some help to sort them out'. On the way in which the patient treated the doctor, Balint notes 'a highly appealing, almost childish confidence'. He also describes his own reactions: 'I could not help responding positively to this apparently sincere and warm appeal. I was aware of its latent homosexual, paranoid nature'. What he foresaw after the first interview is set out as follows: 'Some easing of the tension and an increase of his friendly, somewhat homosexual affection towards me'. The forms to complete were qualitative in content, and served above all to sharpen the therapist's questionings and to bring together the reflection of the participants in the research group. Thus for the indications and the objectives of the psychotherapy, the task was not to set out a scientific prognosis, but to describe the representations and expectations of the therapist, to talk about them within the group, to improve the understanding of the case and to confront these elements with what transpired in the subsequent sessions. Thus, for each session, Balint describes the therapist's forecasts, the setting of the interview, the 'therapeutic interventions given' and those 'thought of but not given', the 'focal aims', the 'outcome of the interview' and the 'afterthoughts' that the interview raised. These forms meant that the therapist, 'in describing his work under these headings, demonstrated the therapeutic process to the working group, and any inconsistencies in his work or his thinking could be seen'.[15] The fact that they existed reflects a desire for thoroughness in the research: ordering observations, fostering a common language among researchers and, as in all research, validating or refuting hypotheses.[16]

Psychotherapies conducted by non-analysts

These also have a 'research-action' dimension, and they combine research and training. In *Psychotherapeutic Techniques in Medicine*, Michael and Enid Balint based their work on research and training seminars organised in the Tavistock Clinic, attended by more than 200 practitioners. Meetings lasted about an hour and a half every two weeks.[17] The seminars were taped and transcribed, as were those involving social workers, on which the book is also partially based. The purpose of the groups was not to describe patients' psychopathologies, but to focus on the technique of the practitioner, and on the interactions between patient and practitioner, so as to define a specific psychotherapy practised by doctors, and by non-analysts more generally.

In Balint groups, the doctor presents a case in spontaneous manner, without notes. For the purposes of the research, and 'to focus the doctor's attention, among other things, on the interplay of emotions between the patient and himself,'[18] one group of doctors used a form similar to that used in the Focal Therapy Workshop. In order to draw the doctor's attention to his counter-transference – to sharpen his questioning and because counter-transference contributes to the patient's symptoms – at the top of the form in bold letters and underlined there were the words 'negative findings must be explicitly stated'. Oddly enough, there were no such instructions for positive findings. Yet Balint did considerable work on the risk of 'mutual seduction' between patient and doctor, which can generate mistaken conclusions on improvements in symptoms, and a failure to detect the real challenges of the case. By way of the form, the group noted the smallest details, on the assumption that this was a way to apprehend unconscious processes under way in the therapeutic relationship. Thus in one case described in *Psychotherapeutic Techniques in Medicine*, under the item 'how the doctor treated the patient', the doctor wrote: 'At this point whilst writing up the report I stopped to make a cup of coffee!!! At first I was grumpy and cross at the nuisance value of this patient . . .'. When the case was presented to the group and in the ensuing discussion, the group concluded that the doctor had avoided the question of sexuality, and linked this omission to his need to make himself a cup of coffee.

Research on the 'flash' technique lasted six years. It was based on the observation that the psychotherapeutic techniques used in general medicine up to that time were in fact very little practised by doctors, and that they resulted in a divide in their practice: the usual medical functioning on the one hand, and psychotherapeutic practices on the other, entailing a risk of equating the practitioner with an analyst, ultimately leading to a sort of 'watered-down psychoanalysis'.[19] The aim of this research was to understand the processes at work and the psychotherapeutic impact of acts performed in the setting of general medicine in everyday practice, where the doctor retained his professional identity. The research had a dual purpose: first, to determine what were the forms of psychotherapeutic practice occurring within a normal general medicine consultation, by focusing on the emergence of 'brief, intense, intimate contacts', and 'peculiar, intense flashes of understanding between doctor and patient'[20] during which patient and doctor were 'tuned in', these being the moments referred to as 'flashes'. The second purpose was to assess the efficacy of this approach. This work was positioned in the continuation of the 'Focal Therapies'. It was influenced by Winnicott's 'Therapeutic Consultation' model. Winnicott was indeed invited to the Focal Therapy Workshop, and Balint referred explicitly to his work in *Six Minutes for the Patient*.

The research group was composed of doctors with a wide experience of the psychotherapeutic techniques initiated by the Balint groups. They had agreed to take part in a research and training group centred on their daily practice. The group comprised eight general practitioners, two psychiatrists and psychotherapists, and three analysts. The cases presented were to be subjected to a systematic regular follow-up for eighteen months (reflecting the ever-present endeavour to assess therapeutic results in the long term). The doctor was to detail his therapeutic plan and the expected results (again reflecting the rule of confronting hypotheses and results, and proceeding from this confrontation). Because this work was centred on a classic consultation in general medicine, the doctor was to specify the 'traditional diagnosis' and the 'overall diagnosis' (i.e. what he perceived of the patient's symptoms, his personality, his expectations and the doctor–patient relationship). The forms used were adapted from those used in the Focal Therapy Workshop. They were altered by the group from the experience gained to suit the object of the research.[21] A questionnaire assessing the patient's state during follow-up (the follow-up form) was also developed.

Interdisciplinarity

Balint thought that the contribution of psychoanalysis to psychotherapies, and more generally to reflection in other disciplines, was considerable. But he was also aware of the limits, and the need for collaboration on an equal footing with other disciplines. This meant that each protagonist needed to be well-acquainted with the manners of thinking of the other areas of knowledge, and the limitations of these different fields. The work conducted by Balint was thus a school of interdisciplinarity: normally speaking each participant retained his own professional identity, while at the same time seeking to understand the other's way of thinking, and drawing on it for his own account. This approach could interest analysts today working in a medical setting or in institutions. On the part of the analyst it requires 'internal inter-disciplinarity',[22] that is to say sufficient interior availability to understand the other's calling, his professional ideals, his manners of thinking, but without losing one's own identity. This internal interdisciplinarity is a difficult exercise, since it requires a temporary decentring in the analyst's manner of listening, and then a return to his position as an analyst. It also needs the person to be easy with his own professional identity, and requires reflection on the assets and the limitations of his own discipline and practice, and on the disciplines and practices of other protagonists.

In the research and training groups that Balint initiated and ran, non-analysts (doctors and social workers) were received on equal footing ('as our equals').[23] Indeed, for Balint, the field of psychoanalysis was restricted despite its undeni-able contributions. He voiced objections on several occasions regarding the illusion of the omniscience of psychoanalysis in the area of psychotherapies, propounded by analysts and shared by those who set out to practise psycho-therapy. This, according to him, could only end in a 'teacher–pupil relation-ship' and a 'poor form of watered-down analytic technique', artificially compromising the professional identity of those practising it. Just as for the training of analysts, he was against any role of leadership for the analysts, whether in Balint groups or within research and training groups; he was also against any alienating identification with the ideals of psychoanalysis.[24]

Balint considered that the various techniques and criteria of psychoanalysis were not applicable indiscriminately to all types of psychotherapy. Other approaches, he thought, had a lot to teach psychoanalysts, and were more suitable. Given the settings in which the psychoanalytic cures and psycho-therapies take place, that is to say a two-person relationship that is 'insulated', limited in time, probably with regular encounters between patient and therapist, he thought that psychoanalysts 'know but little about the therapeutic possibilities and the professional hazards' of the practice of non-analysts. Doctors have an ongoing relationship, unlikely to be limited in time, with their patients. The frequency of encounters is variable. They often care for the whole family, and they also examine the patient, thus coming into contact with his body, and they of course prescribe. He considered that this meant that there was a need for the elaboration of a specifically tailored psychotherapeutic technique, using the contributions of psychoanalysis. He thought that these contributions were at once considerable and limited. Psychoanalysts needed to realise that, when they agreed to train doctors or other non-analysts, they were dealing with something of which they had poorer knowledge than they did of the psychoanalytic technique.[25] They could, however, contribute very usefully if, in their work with doctors, they focused on the issue of counter-transference. And although the doctors were considered 'as our equals'[26] in this work, the analysts could detect the unconscious in dealings within these research and training seminars, that is to say the counter-transferences of the practitioner and his 'apostolic function',[27] so that it was then possible to intervene according to what was observed.

Balint's consideration of the place of analysts in pluri-disciplinary work with doctors has relevance today: first, in relation to the 'talking groups' involving caregivers or social workers that they run, and, second, in relation to the research and training processes conducted jointly with doctors on issues such as medical ethics.[28]

Theoretical issues with present-day relevance

The issues broached by Balint on the subject of brief psychotherapies follow on from the questions raised by the classic psychoanalytic cure, and can be seen as belonging to debate within the psychoanalytical movement.

Transmission of a mode of clinical practice

In his writings on psychoanalytical cures, Balint only uses clinical vignettes. He is at pains, however, to set out these clinical cases exhaustively, or at least meaningfully, when dealing with the medical sphere and brief psychotherapies, and hence 'applied psychoanalysis', applying what he saw as a research approach. His clinical cases, faithfully transcribed from accounts dictated to his secretary, from notes made during training seminars, or from recordings of certain group sessions,[29] provide a significant amount of material, and a possible model for a qualitative approach in the area of psychopathology of the '*cas au singulier*'[30] or 'single case' type, widely used today in a large body of research. Indeed, Balint describes the different actors involved in a case (the doctor or psychotherapist, the patient, his or her entourage, the training seminar, the institutional setting). He describes his work of elaboration, his hypotheses, his interpretations, the interventions he envisaged but did not talk about, the way the therapeutic relationship evolved, the relationships among the different members of the training group and the follow-up. This is how he produced 'single cases' that could be passed on to others, as potential models for his theoretical reflection, thus enabling his thinking to be traced and followed, and even refuted.

The place of the psychotherapies in relation to psychoanalysis

Balint positions his 'focal psychotherapy' as an extension of psychoanalysis. He does, however, describe a specific place for psychotherapies in relation to psychoanalysis in instances where the setting and the therapeutic objectives differ markedly from psychoanalytical practice. The different psychoanalytical approaches all have their particular value. The technical criteria of psychoanalysis cannot be applied in all situations. Balint's intention was to develop new psychoanalytical techniques in collaboration with non-analysts and then to circulate them. But he also wanted to raise interest for psychotherapies among psychoanalysts, and he deplored their lack of openness towards domains other than 'straight' psychoanalysis, and their absence of curiosity. Better understanding and better knowledge of other techniques could, he thought, contribute to their clinical practice and to psychoanalytical theory. Psychoanalysts, with their specific tools, could assist in the process of elaboration of these other techniques.

In *Psychotherapeutic Techniques in Medicine*, Balint describes different types of psychotherapy in the light of two aspects: what he calls the 'setting', and the therapeutic aims. Thus the results derived from psychoanalysis and those derived from group therapy, even if it is of the psychoanalytical type, are very different. The two approaches do not address the same level of the psyche, because of the setting. In the first instance 'the patient is definitely less neurotic (or psychotic) but perhaps not necessarily really mature', while in the second instance 'the patient is not necessarily less neurotic, but inevitably more mature'. In the psychoanalytical process 'the patient receives full and undivided attention in a very close and intense two-person relationship', which may favour regressive tendencies. In group therapy 'every patient must accustom himself to the idea of fair shares' with fellow members of the group, giving help at times, and at least discovering what it is to take an interest in others. In certain cases 'the therapist's chief attention is upon readjusting the patient's external behaviour with important people in his environment; the focus of the work is on what the patient does and why he does it, and the aim is to help him to behave differently'. In other cases, 'the therapeutic aim is to help the patient readjust some of his internal problems; the therapist concentrates the work on the patient's intra-psychic problems and pays less attention to how these internal problems affect the patient's behaviour'. The two aims are often intertwined. Balint was also interested in the different interview techniques (psychological and psychiatric), in the diagnostic interview as practised by doctors, psychiatrists and psychologists, and in the resulting psychotherapeutic repercussions. He deplored the fact that psychoanalysts showed no interest in this issue, whether for themselves or for other professions.

These differentiations between different psychotherapeutic approaches, the concern that analysts should be more open to experiences from outside the analytical sphere, and that the other professions should be more open to psychoanalysis, in no way prevent consistency and fine-tuning in what is offered to the patient, or in integrating the implications of these stances. This enables the therapist to avoid being caught up in a single-minded system, and, in practice, it avoids one and the same therapist taking it upon himself to intervene at different levels. This supposes sufficient mental flexibility on the part of the therapist, but it also involves a risk of confusion. Therefore the therapist needs wide prior experience in his own discipline, and he needs to have given adequate consideration to his own professional identity, so as to refrain from negation or idealisation in relation to his practice and his discipline. He also needs to be able to call upon different reference models, and to identify them as accurately as possible. It follows that he needs to understand the reasons for his choices within the therapeutic relationship, and to assess the consequences for the continuation of the psychotherapy. Balint's clinical theory is particularly interesting today because we are faced with a vast, rather vague constellation coming under the name of 'psychotherapy', ill-defined in the medical and educational world, in society and among patients; or alternatively we are confronted with closed-shop schools of thought offering a psychotherapeutic approach claiming to be exhaustive and exclusive.

The psychotherapeutic process

As a follow-up to his reflection on the psychoanalytic cure, Balint wanted to identify and gain a better understanding of the factors determining change in the therapeutic process. He also wanted to ascertain whether the therapeutic process could lead to a 'considerable though limited change' in a patient's personality.[31]

He hoped to generate a process of change for the patients he was following in focal psychotherapy by way of a transference relationship centred on the 'here-and-now' of the object-relation, and on what he considered as the main or 'focal' conflict in the patient. Thus Mr Baker, a case presented in *Focal Psychotherapy*, was a patient suffering from 'severe jealousy paranoia'. After the second interview, Balint described the focal objectives as follows:

> In the first part of the interview I thought I had found it in the feelings of guilt caused by his triumph over his homosexual rivals [. . .] But it is quite possible that this will prove to be too ambitious. In this case, a secondary aim might be to enable him in the transference to find a man with whom he can share his wife (symbolically).

In order to analyse the therapeutic process, he differentiates the various interventions of the analyst: CO (current observations): 'the interpretation is based exclusively or predominantly on current observations in the therapeutic situation', that is to say that the analyst bases himself first of all on experience acquired in other cases; M (mixed): 'the basis of the interpretation could not be identified with certainty'; P Psa K (pre-existing psychoanalytic knowledge): 'the interpretation is based exclusively or predominantly on pre-existing psychoanalytic knowledge, which may in some cases mean only preconceived ideas, prejudices, or unproven biases, hypotheses, or wishful thinking held by the therapist'; ID (independent discovery by the patient). Underpinning this arbitrary classification, and his pseudo-scientific attempt to quantify these different types of interpretation during psychotherapy in the form of percentages, there is a more interesting issue: what is the function of the various interventions by the psychoanalyst in the course of the psychotherapeutic process, and which are those that lead to change?

This issue is brought up on the subject of the 'flash' technique,[32] the most intensive form of focal psychotherapy, practised by non-analysts. The place of the 'flash' technique and its content are of interest to analysts, in that this practice casts light on elements enabling interpretation or operating changes in the patient's subjective position. The approach, which Balint positions explicitly as following on from the focal therapy technique,[33] aims to go further in the use of the object-relationship in transference, and its links with the arrival of a sudden clue to interpretation. *Six Minutes for the Patient* only provides a phenomenological description of the 'flash' technique. In the therapeutic process, the patient 'uses the doctor and is in control of the pace and content of the therapy'. Here Balint is in line with his theories on the psychoanalytic cure where the analyst is above all 'a provider of time and milieu'.[34] The flash provides a fertile, creative moment of empathy between the patient and the therapist, a moment of co-construction and a moment of truth that the patient can use if he so wishes. It is a 'brief, intense, intimate contact between doctor and patient' which enables a change in the subjective position of the patient. At these moments, patient and doctor are 'tuned in'. This special moment enables the patient to discover things about himself. It calls on the doctor's ability for intuition, and on elements of identification between doctor and patient[35] (distinct from moments of complicity). The flash technique, like focal psychotherapy, is centred on the patient's focal conflict and on the here-and-now of the session. It requires 'selective attention' by the therapist, rather than 'evenly poised' attention. Indeed, in focal psychotherapy, the therapist uses 'selective neglect' alongside 'selective attention', that is to say he focuses his attention on psychic material that is linked to the chosen focus. 'Of all that the patient offers, only those aspects are interpreted that facilitate and enhance the work on the chosen focus'.

What is it that makes up the 'flash' technique, and what are its psychic mechanisms? This was not clearly theorised by Balint. It seems to me that the 'flash' occurs when a 'potential space', an 'area of transitional phenomena' is created between the doctor and the patient.[36] The flash is generated by the experience of a moment when the patient and the doctor are very close to what Winnicott calls the 'creative impulse'.[37] The interpretation then becomes a 'transitional object'. In Winnicott's *Therapeutic Consultations in Child Psychiatry*[38] it appears to arise from a moment of 'mutual experience' between the analyst and the child or adolescent, involving the body in its most intimate relationships with the space of dreams, the unconscious, and 'creative impulse'. The 'squiggle' technique used by Winnicott in his therapeutic consultations with children enables contact to be made with the 'stuff of dreams' and an isolated, intense psychoanalytic encounter between the child and the therapist. Its nature is detailed by Winnicott: 'From the drawings of a child and of the child and myself one can find one way of making the case come alive. It is almost as if the child, through the drawings, is alongside me, and to some extent taking part in describing the case.' Sometimes Winnicott completes a 'squiggle' with his eyes shut. He is then verging on the experience of the unconscious and the 'creative impulse', which he defines as follows:

> The creative impulse is therefore something [. . .] that is present when anyone [. . .] looks in a healthy way at anything or does anything deliberately, such as making a mess with faeces or prolonging the act of crying to enjoy a musical sound. It is present as much in the moment-by-moment living of a backward child who is enjoying breathing as it is in the inspiration of an architect.[39]

O. Mannoni in 'La férule'[40] also describes what it is that enables interpretation to arise, how it is generated by counter-transference, from associations and also from the involvement of the analyst's body. In the course of a very difficult and exasperating cure, he found himself looking at the cane[41] on his desk while his female patient was once again compulsively 'raising her legs in indecent fashion, throwing her bag and handkerchief to the ceiling and swearing'. This gave rise to a series of associations and bodily acts arising from an identification with the patient, in which were intermingled his own childhood memories, a reference to Sartre[42] who as a child pulled faces in front of the mirror when he was overtaken by shame, and remembrances of himself, finding himself one evening compulsively saying out loud a meaningless sentence while reading Gombrowicz.[43] The idea that this patient was in fact playing out her shame then hit him. This discovery enabled Mannoni to re-centre his attention in the cure, although he did not tell the patient his interpretation. As if in a 'flash', the interpretation arose[44] when the space of the session formed a 'potential space' for the analyst, and this lasted beyond the session.

The question of the setting

In the course of Mr Baker's psychotherapy Balint was very flexible with the setting in which the session took place. The frequency varied. The patient used the doctor, and determined the frequency and the content of the therapeutic work.[45] The interval between sessions ranged from three days (when the patient asked to be seen again quickly) to several weeks, and at other times it was regular. Thus at the second session the patient asked for time to reflect because it became clear that he did not have the same plans for the therapy as the therapist. He was expecting a treatment of his symptoms lasting five or six sessions, during which he could use Balint as a 'sounding board', while Balint was interested in 'finding out what had happened to him'. These liberties with the setting can in some cases be risky, in particular when they encourage an entrenchment of the defences, and non-elaborated transferences or counter-transferences, or when the flexibility of the setting in fact results from non-identified enactment. In Mr Baker's case the spacing out of sessions was sometimes linked to counter-transference by the analyst, and his assessment of the psychotherapeutic potential. The interest of this case lies in the frankness and the clarity with which these elements are set out by Balint, as well as the doubts and questionings he entertained. Thus at the end of the thirteenth session, when the issue of terminating the sessions was raised following some progress in the symptoms, for the first time Mr Baker asked Balint if his treatment would really free him from his obsessive ruminations.

> I got somewhat frightened, because this was a straightforward request for proper analysis which, in view of his illness and of the distance he had to travel to London, is not a very practical proposition. I thought it best to temporise, and so I proposed that we should use the impending break as a kind of test period to see how much he had gained and then we would decide this most important issue in the light of his state after the break. This he readily accepted.

After the session, Balint wondered if the way the patient had questioned him on his future was not 'a displacement onto me of his urge to torment people'. 'He does not know, for the first time in this treatment, what to expect'. Given the later aggravation of the patient's state and his repeated acting-out, Balint wondered if it was the result of his own refusal to commit himself to a long therapy, and his proposal to discontinue the treatment. At the same time he was uncertain about the causes of this aggravation: was it a result of transference by the patient, or a result of his own counter-transference? On reading this case, we can wonder about the analyst's decision. Was it perceived by the patient as an acting-in of the psychoanalyst, to which he responded?

Balint appears to partially avoid this question. Yet several times he clearly pinpoints the effects of his counter-transferences or his hesitations on the course of the psychotherapy.[46]

Since psychoanalytical theory should concern itself with 'two-person, three-person, four-person psychology', Balint defines this mode of practice via the case of Mr Baker (and also using cases presented by doctors). He readily meets Mr Baker's wife, either on request from the patient or from his wife, or on his own initiative, and he also responds to requests from the treating physician. This means that attention needs to be paid to the transference relationship with the patient, and also to the way in which transference circulates among family and caregivers, and to the part played by their expectations within the transference and counter-transference relationships. Indeed, Balint wonders about the nature of the relationship he entertains with Mr Baker's doctor, about his wavering confidence when the patient's state deteriorates and its incidence on the psychotherapeutic process. At the very first encounter, Balint offered to meet Mr Baker's wife, who had remained in the waiting room. He does not clearly specify the reasons. However, there appear to be three elements in this decision. Balint wanted to gain insight into the relationship between the patient and his wife, and to ascertain how far the patient could rely on his familiar environment. This was also a concern with Winnicott. The quality of the family and social environment and their ties with the patient were, in his view, a factor for progress, and assessing them was part of the decision whether or not to undertake a long psychotherapy. This concern is also seen among psychotherapists working in the medical sphere, since the sustaining of mutual recognition between the patient and his entourage and the quality of the trust that they can establish among themselves are important elements in enabling the patient to cope with the experience of his illness in the best possible manner. In addition, Balint probably wanted to establish a therapeutic relationship with the patient's wife, and, in the 'here-and-now' of the session, finally materialise one of his 'focal aims': in the transference, finding 'a man with whom he can share his wife (symbolically)'. Thus in the tenth session, without it being planned, the patient came accompanied by his wife, and Balint interviewed her briefly. One of the interpretations envisaged, but not communicated to the patient, was as follows: 'I could have interpreted the appearance of his wife as his attempt at sharing her with me and as a sign of growing confidence both in himself and in me that this could happen.'

The need to involve several protagonists in the here-and-now of the session raises numerous theoretical problems. This practice is today one that is used by psychoanalysts in the medical sphere, in institutions or in family therapies. Psychoanalysts have above all approached it via psychoanalytical family therapies or via reflections on the institution,[47] along with other theoretical elaborations such as the group or family 'psychic apparatus' viewed as an intermediate psychic construction within which unconscious communication occurs, ordered around a primary psyche. These theorisations do not exist in Balint, even if, in the Balint groups, he assimilates the presentation of a case by a doctor to 'the manifest content of a dream'.[48] He focuses more on the object-relationship and the here-and-now of the session or of the group situation. Just as the patient's acting-out can be viewed as free association, in brief psychotherapies the analyst's acting-in can also be seen as interpretation. Thus in the fifteenth session, Mr and Mrs Baker arrived for the appointment one hour late. Balint received them and considered that this attitude amounted to an interpretation, based on 'current observation'. 'Translated into words, what the therapist "said" by his behaviour could run: "In spite of your resistance, I think you need therapy right now. Luckily I am free, so here I am to listen to you".'

Notes

1 See also Chapter 5 in this book.
2 M. and E. Balint, *Psychotherapeutic Techniques in Medicine* (London: Tavistock Publications, 1961).
3 Better known as Balint groups.
4 This research was continued by M. Balint until his death, and then by E. Balint. *Six Minutes for the Patient* is a collective work coordinated by E. Balint and J. S. Norell, published in 1973 (London: Tavistock Publications).
5 D. H. Malan, *A Study of Brief Psychotherapy* (London: Tavistock Publications, 1963).
6 M. Balint, P. Ornstein and E. Balint, *Focal Psychology* (London: Tavistock Publications, 1972). P. Ornstein sustained regular exchanges with M. Balint from 1956. He was a psychiatrist and a psychoanalyst, and lectured in Cincinnati University in the USA where M. Balint was guest professor.
7 On this type of practice, see, for instance, K. N. De Witt, Nancy B. Kaltreider, D. S. Weiss and M. J. Horowitz, 'Judging change in psychotherapy', *Archives of General Psychiatry* 40 (1983): 1121–8; L. Luborski, 'Recurrent momentary forgetting, its content and its context' in M. J. Horowitz (ed.), *Psychodynamics and Cognition* (Chicago, IL: University of Chicago Press, 1988), pp. 223–52.
8 This is an intentional use of terminology adopted by INSERM. See INSERM, *La recherche action en santé* (Paris: Documentation Française, 1988).
9 Balint *et al.*, *Focal Psychotherapy*.
10 See M. Moreau-Ricaud, *Michael Balint: Le renouveau de l'école de Budapest* (Ramonville Sainte-Agne: Erès, 2000).
11 In Balint *et al.*, *Focal Psychotherapy*.
12 The story of these forms is narrated in M. and E. Balint, *Psychotherapeutic Techniques in Medicine* and in Balint and Norell, *Six Minutes for the Patient*.
13 Balint *et al.*, *Focal Psychotherapy*.
14 This term is also used by Winnicott.
15 Balint *et al.*, *Focal Psychotherapy*.
16 *Ibid.*

17 For further details on this organisation, see Chapter 5 in this book.
18 M. and E. Balint, *Psychotherapeutic Techniques in Medicine*.
19 This phrase is used by M. Balint in Balint and Norell, *Six Minutes for the Patient*. In my opinion this risk is one of the weaknesses of Balint groups, and the pitfall has not always been avoided.
20 The phrase is used by E. Balint in Balint and Norell, *Six Minutes for the Patient*.
21 All the forms designed by Balint and his research teams evolved with use. This mode of research, consisting in starting from one or several cases to refine hypotheses and gradually develop tools, is termed 'grounded theory' by researchers in the social sciences (B. G. Glaser and A. L. Strauss, *The Discovery of Grounded Theory*, Vol. 1 (Chicago, IL: Aldine, 1967)). Today it is recognised as one possible approach in qualitative research in medicine.
22 A phrase used by B. Virole in a talk to the Société de Psychanalyse Freudienne.
23 This is referred to several times by Balint, in particular in *Psychotherapeutic Techniques in Medicine*.
24 Nevertheless, Balint groups did not escape the bias denounced by Balint, and often trained doctors, paramedics or social workers who wanted to imitate analysts; this resulted in a divide in their professional practices if they did not actually become analysts themselves. See also Chapter 5 in this book.
25 M. Balint, 'Psycho-analysis and medical practice', *International Journal of Psychoanalysis* 47 (1966): 54–9.
26 This supposes a shared research process, and the idea that each profession learns from the other, even within training seminars of the Balint group type. The notions of equality between psychoanalysts and doctors, and of the 'training-cum-research' method, were later neglected when Balint groups developed towards a focus on training, which implies that the relationship between analysts and group participants is necessarily unequal, and this is indeed reflected in the use of the word 'leader' to refer to the analysts, and the 'conversion' of participants to the 'watered-down form of psychoanalytic technique'.
27 In *The Doctor, His Patient and the Illness* (London: Churchill Livingstone, 2000), Balint defines the 'apostolic function' of the doctor as follows: 'Apostolic mission or function means in the first place that every doctor has a vague, but almost unshakably firm idea of how a patient ought to behave when ill [. . .] It was almost as if every doctor had revealed knowledge of what was right and what was wrong for patients to expect and to endure, and further, as if he had a sacred duty to convert to his faith all the ignorant and unbelieving among his patients.'
28 Underpinning the demand from doctors and caregivers for ethical discussion on cases encountered in their practice (which should be differentiated from the rulings of the National Ethics Committee, which belong to the sphere of deontology), there was also the desire to reflect on their apostolic function, on the ever-present need for their assessment and judgement, and on the conflicts of values with which they were confronted. Within the Société Française de Thérapeutique du Généraliste I created the Groupe de Réflexion Médicale au Quotidien (i.e. reflecting on day-to-day medicine), which is a training and research group assembling doctors, psycho-analysts, philosophers and legal experts, centred on the ethical issues raised by cases presented by the doctors. This group encouraged each participant to confront the limitations encountered in his or her particular domain, and likewise encoura-ged new theoretical openings, which of course had an impact on the professional identity of each. On the subject of the analyst in the group, at this time I wrote: 'Reflection on the "ethical act" in medicine highlights the different logics within

which both doctors and patients are enclosed. Ethical reflection puts the respective merits of scientific advances, and of the unconscious, social or economic foundations of the identities of patient and caregiver in their right place, making it possible to pinpoint the limits of the medical sphere, and the different logics (legal, sociological, institutional, economic, scientific or unconscious) in which the patient and the doctor find themselves. The psychoanalyst can but note the scientific, legal, sociological, institutional and economic foundations of the ethical act, and accept the confrontation, in the same manner as the other participants in the group, and this has a lot to offer him or her. What he or she can however contribute to reflection by the doctor is insight into the unconscious foundations of the ethical act' (H. Oppenheim-Gluckman, 'Psychanalyse et ethique', *Panoramiques* 22 (1995): 107–12).

29 In *The Doctor, His Patient and the Illness*, *Psychotherapeutic Techniques in Medicine*, *Six Minutes for the Patient* and *Focal Psychotherapy*.

30 D. Widlocher, 'Le cas au singulier', *Nouvelle Revue de Psychanalyse* 42 (1990): 285–302.

31 Balint used this expression not on the subject of patients, but on the subject of the aims of the Balint groups, talking of the 'considerable though limited change in the doctor's personality' (see Chapter 5 in this book). I have intentionally used the same phrase here because this concern with changes of personality that are 'considerable though limited' pervades his questionings on the brief psychotherapies and the patient care provided by doctors and other non-analysts.

32 Balint and Norell, *Six Minutes for the Patient*.

33 In the only chapter he wrote in Balint and Norell, *Six Minutes for the Patient*.

34 See Chapter 2 in this book.

35 See also D. W. Winnicott, *Therapeutic Consultations in Child Psychiatry* (London: Karnac Books, 1996). Winnicott notes that the therapeutic consultation requires an identification between patient and therapist, but that the therapist should not lose his own identity.

36 D. W. Winnicott, 'Transitional objects and transitional phenomena' in *Playing and Reality* (London: Routledge, 1989), pp. 1–25.

37 D. W. Winnicott, 'Creativity and its origins' in *Playing and Reality*, pp. 65–85.

38 D. W. Winnicott, *Therapeutic Consultations in Child Psychiatry* (London: Karnac Books, 1996).

39 'Creativity and its origins' in Winnicott, *Playing and Reality*.

40 In O. Mannoni, *Ça n'empêche pas d'exister* (Paris: Le Seuil, 1982), pp. 63–84.

41 The word *férule* in French refers to a wood and leather instrument for punishing naughty schoolchildren, fairly close to the 'cane' or 'ruler' in English schools of the time.

42 French writer.

43 Polish writer.

44 For Mannoni, any interpretation is a creation.

45 There were twenty-seven sessions over a period of fifteen months, and then a period of follow-up with exchange of letters and three sessions.

46 Fifteenth session: 'And lastly, there is an evident transference interpretation: if I propose to terminate the treatment he produces new and alarming symptoms. Very likely, this was one of the determining factors in his homosexual experiences.' Seventeenth session: 'The therapist was uncertain how to understand this serious change. The less sombre idea would be to consider the deterioration as a violent response to the therapist's acceptance that the treatment was about to terminate;

the change for the worse would then be a bitter punishment of the therapist's attempt at abandoning his patient. The other, more ominous, possibility was to consider the paranoid illness as an irresistibly progressing process [. . .] In the next following session, this hesitant, uncertain attitude on the part of the therapist is clearly observable.'

47 D. Anzieu, 'L'illusion groupale', *Nouvelle Revue de la Psychanalyse* 4 (1971): 73–93; R. Kaës (ed.), *L'institution et les institutions, études psychanalytiques* (Paris: Dunod, 1988); A. Ruffiot (ed.), *La thérapie familiale psychanalytique* (Paris: Dunod, 1981).
48 M. Balint, 'Psycho-analysis and medical practice', *International Journal of Psychoanalysis* 47 (1966): 54–62.

Chapter 5

The medical sphere: the Balint groups

Balint is above all known for his work in the medical sphere, and in particular the training of general practitioners. Balint group became the generic term to refer to 'talking' groups of professionals centred on the patient–caregiver relationship, whatever their practice. Since 1974 there has been an International Balint Federation gathering some forty national associations.[1]

The organisation of this work

Balint had complex relationships with his family history and with his origins. In adolescence and early adulthood, he broke away from Judaism, and converted to Unitarianism, and he changed his family name, Bergsmann, to adopt the name of Balint, which is a typically Hungarian name. He was always very secretive about his private life, the reasons for his conversion and the break away from his origins.[2] In addition to the fact that his father was a general practitioner in Hungary, and Balint's own initial scientific and medical training, his interest in raising awareness towards the unconscious and subjective aspects of their practice among general practitioners derived from the preoccupations of the Hungarian Psychoanalytic Society. In Budapest, following on from Ferenczi, he led seminars for doctors which included theoretical contributions. An article such as the 'Crisis of medical practice'[3] is exemplary of this period (around the 1930s). This text is the viewpoint of an enlightened doctor on medical practice, on the new problems encountered by doctors in the context of the medical institution in Hungary, the place of the medical institution in society, the development of new knowledge, the capitalist economic context and the development of the pharmaceutical industry. The training methods in the Hungarian Psychoanalytic Society were to profoundly influence the content and the approaches used in Balint groups.

There are several descriptions of the history and implementation of this work.[4] Following on from the group supervision conducted with social workers ('case-workers') catering for couples encountering difficulties – work that was initiated by Enid Balint in the 1950s and in which Balint participated – he decided to launch training seminars for general practitioners. General practitioners had already been receiving teaching on psychotherapy over the previous twenty years in the Tavistock Clinic, but Balint considered that this teaching did not enable any real evolution in the professional practice of doctors, because it was based on the delivery of psychopathological knowledge and on the classic models of psychiatry and psychotherapy. For Balint, the training of doctors in the patient–doctor relationship should be based on practical skills rather than theoretical knowledge. He therefore proposed not to *teach*, but to *train* doctors, using methods based on group techniques and the experience already acquired with the social workers. The first doctors were recruited through the medical press via an advertisement announcing an 'introductory course in psychotherapy for general practitioners'.[5] The first seminars gathered eight to twelve practitioners for two hours a week. One of the doctors presented a case, which was discussed in the group, with no supporting written material. The doctor could nevertheless use his clinical notes as an 'aide-mémoire' (reminder). A case once presented could be followed up and re-discussed at a later stage. In certain groups cases were chosen randomly (the second patient in yesterday's consultation, for example). These groups lasted over two or three years, and during this time the doctors were to continue their practice in general medicine. Today, the groups last much longer, and may have no limitation in time. This raises clinical issues. Is there not a risk that the group might become an enclosed space, where the participants are caught up in a defensive 'group fantasy or group illusion' and regressive movements? Groups with unlimited duration appeared in Balint's lifetime in the Tavistock Clinic. In addition, a support and follow-up group was offered after the end of the training for participants who were interested. Was this a recognition of the 'addiction' of general practitioners taking part? Was this addiction generated by the training system itself, and the nature of transferences and identifications in the groups? Or was there an inability for mourning processes in some doctors, which could very well have an impact on their relationships with their patients? The reasons motivating the formation of this support group and its pitfalls do not seem to have been analysed by Balint.

At the start, in Balint groups, teaching was not completely absent. The group sessions centred on a case were backed up by a lecture on psychoanalytic theory. Those who wished could also have individual supervision with 'consultants' in the Tavistock Clinic, different from the person in charge of the group. This was later discontinued because of the lack of results.[6] Is this because, as for psychoanalysts, the 'supervising instructor' was experienced as a mentor by the doctors, implicating elements of rivalry and submission on their part, as shown in certain cases reported in *The Doctor, His Patient and the Illness*? Or is it because, by favouring a process of identification with the supervisor, this supervision also favoured the temptation to comply with the psychoanalytic model? A 'consultant', psychiatrist in the Tavistock Clinic, could be consulted by the patient for his opinion, or a psychologist could be asked for a psychological evaluation using tests. The results of these consultations and evaluations were reported to the group. The theme of the first seminars was the medication usually prescribed by practitioners. This then raised the question of the 'drug "doctor"', in other words the question of how the doctor 'prescribes himself', which was to be a major theme in Balint groups. With respect to medical practice and its differences with psychoanalytic practice, the choice of this theme and the shift from prescribing medication to prescribing the doctor amount to an interesting dynamic, if it is set against the fact that the founding element in psychoanalysis was the renunciation of cocaine and the therapeutic object, that is to say medication.[7]

The seminars were research and training seminars. Balint wanted to avoid the teacher–pupil relationship between the doctors and the group leader, and this links up with his concerns about the training of analysts and the fact that he thought it was for the doctors to define the psychotherapy methods best suited to their practice.[8] In this perspective he suggested doctors taking part in his groups should read his texts before publication,[9] which is an interesting research approach providing useful information, whereby those who are the subject of the research are also active agents. This practice, which also had its ethical reasons, is also used today in research in the area of psychopathology.

In *The Doctor, His Patient and the Illness*, Balint notes that the frequentation of the seminars in the first year was 'very good (90–95%)'. Reality was, however, more complex. Very soon, as the seminars unfolded, the training aspect took precedence over the research aspect, and from the outset there were quite a number of dropouts, leaving a stable and enthusiastic core group contributing actively to the research work. For Balint, psychotherapeutic skills are only acquired by discovering 'hard facts', which may not always be pleasant, on one's own limitations and those of others. Crisis in a group is therefore inevitable, and also necessary for the evolution of participants and leader. As early as his article published in 1954,[10] and later in *The Doctor, His Patient and the Illness*, he describes numerous reasons for the frequent crisis and deadlock in the groups. He reflected at length on the unconscious processes at work there, although he never explicitly refers to them. Crises that are difficult to overcome occur when the mutual identifications between participants are no longer strong enough, and when this is not adequately perceived by the group leader. This leads to withdrawal and a tendency to isolate among members of the group, and to drop out if the group is unable to overcome the crisis. The challenges for the group proposed by the leader can also be too great for the participants. However, the absence of any crisis is worrying. It reflects defensive elements, and the group and its leader then run the risk of degenerating into a 'mutual admiration society'. The leader's attitude is very important. It can generate crisis if it is too rigid or embodies a position of possession of knowledge and control. His attitude also informs participants in the group, because it embodies, in the 'here-and-now' of the group, attitudes and skills towards their own patients that he wants to teach the doctors.

From 1954[11] Balint was concerned about the very numerous dropouts of doctors from the training. Out of thirty-six general practitioners who followed the first sessions, fifteen continued until the end, and 60 per cent abandoned in the first year. This recurred fairly often. In 1964, 223 doctors took part in the training. The technique proposed aimed to achieve a 'considerable though limited change in the doctor's personality'. There was no therapeutic objective, nor was it an academic training. The experience was therefore not well perceived by numerous practitioners, irrespective of their qualities. Their departure in some cases signalled a defensive mode that had become necessary. In a second stage Balint therefore tried to make a more suitable selection of doctors for the training. *A Study of Doctors* is devoted to the evaluation of the training offered, and the audience to which it is suited. 'Training medical students in psychotherapy'[12] raises the question of the inclusion of Balint groups in medical curricula, and the way this might be done.[13] Since the training offered by Balint leads to 'considerable though limited change in the doctor's personality', it cannot cater for all indiscriminately. With his team, Balint, using typologies derived from observation of the sessions, tried to identify the doctors liable to draw benefit from it and others for whom it would not be suitable. Each doctor was offered a 'mutual selection interview' with the group leader or another analyst before the start of the training. The idea of 'mutual selection' rather than selection by those in charge of the group again shows the desire to work on equal, peer-to-peer footing with the doctors. In *A Study of Doctors*, Balint notes with satisfaction that the conclusions of the two parties are often convergent after the interview. This book describes research aimed at creating a typological evaluation grid for practitioners, and also to assess the relevance of the 'mutual selection interviews'. Despite this work, it was difficult to apprehend the representativeness of the doctors attending the training seminars in relation to general practitioners as a whole, and therefore to determine whether this type of training could be included in their basic curriculum. *A Study of Doctors* and 'Training medical students in psychotherapy' show that Balint entertained certain doubts as to the scope for offering his training to all doctors. It appeared more suitable for a few selected candidates. The changes it causes as a result of confrontation with the person's own limits and the questioning of his caregiving ideal do not suit all doctors, irrespective of their scientific, technical or academic qualities. With medical students, still changing and maturing, he offered an awareness-raising course for understanding psychotherapy, and the organisation of Balint groups solely for a certain number selected by individual interview.

What is staged in a Balint group?

In 'Psychoanalysis and medical practice',[14] Balint differentiates two types of proposal for doctors: his own proposal and that of a 'post-graduate education for general practitioners and non-psychiatrist specialists in psychiatry or psychotherapy'. In the first instance, the analyst is in the position of an analyst focusing on practitioners' counter-transference, in the second the analyst is in the position of a teacher. The specificity of Balint groups extends beyond this first differentiation. In contrast to what is often said, the aim of a Balint group is not the doctor–patient relationship, but the unconscious discourse of the doctor setting out his case in its relationship to the patient and to the illness, and more broadly to the medical sphere as a whole. What is worked on is, first, the way in which, through the doctor–patient relationship, the illness and the medical sphere function as primitive objects for the doctor (and for the patient), and, second, the way in which these are related to the doctor's ideals, 'apostolic function' and identifications. This relates to the 'considerable though limited change in the doctor's personality'. Changes occur as a result of the repeated encounters between the discourse of the doctor, that of the group, and that of the leader, irrespective of whether the doctor is the one presenting the case or a group participant reacting to a case presented by a colleague. For Balint, the discourse of the doctor is akin to 'manifest dream-content'.[15] This remark could be generalised to other discourse within the group. Indeed, the work is not only on the counter-transferences of the doctor, but on numerous counter-transferences and discourses: that of the doctor on the patient, the effects it produces on the group and the leader, who also produce discourse that has effects on the discourse of the doctor, his subjective position and even on the subjective position of all the group participants. In the very detailed, often exhaustive case descriptions in *The Doctor, His Patient and the Illness*, the focus is on the relationships among several protagonists all functioning as an object for one another, and confronted with the illness and the medical sphere as objects. These protagonists are the doctor, his patient (absent, and the pretext for discourse), the group, its participants and its leader. Sometimes others may intervene, even if they are physically absent from the group: the institution and its history and the way in which these interfere in the history of the group and its reactions, the supervising instructor who sees the doctor separately, sometimes a consultant from the Tavistock Clinic or a specialist doctor. They all have a role in the elaboration of the case, in its evolution and in its construction. Balint does not deliberately make explicit references to a group theory. This stance is clearly explained in 'Psychoanalysis and medical practice', where he writes:

> Here a note of warning. The technique of interpretation in the setting of the training seminar is, of course, different both from the technique of analytic interpretation conditioned by the setting of the analytic situation and from the technique of group interpretation which is conditioned by the setting of the therapeutic group. The chief difference perhaps is that, in the two therapeutic situations, the aim of the interpretation is to uncover some content of the unconscious, for instance, the motivation for a particular form of behaviour. This of necessity tends to create an inequality between therapist and his patient and stimulates thereby the emergence and transference of primitive, childish emotions. In the setting of our training seminars, one of our main considerations is to preserve the dignity, the independence and the mature responsibility of the participating doctors, without which they cannot function as full members of the research team. Our interpretations, therefore, are hardly ever concerned with the hidden motivation of the doctor's therapeutic behaviour, a sphere which we have come to call his 'private transference'. This remains untouched in the same way as his private life. What we are concerned with is his 'public transference', that is, the part of his professional work that, by his reporting and by his participation in the discussion, has become known to all members of the seminar. And even here our aim is first and foremost to enable him to make discoveries on his own, and we therefore use direct interpretation very sparingly.

However, the way in which cases are presented, and their evolution and the manner in which the group is conducted, draw on the 'Multi-Body Psychology' theory, and institutional and group theory. If we return to what Balint writes on group psychotherapy,[16] analysing the cases he presents, it appears clearly that the evolution among doctors occurs as a result of numerous identifications generated by the group. The group enables them to have a glimpse of a multitude of different actions and positions, and outcomes that are more flexible in relation to their ideals and their controlling situation. It also enables them to be more aware of their limitations and better able to accept them. Thus the group helps the doctor to acquire more internal flexibility by widening the scope of representations on the case presented, and thus the range of his own representations. This evolution is only possible if the leader of the group, with whom the participants identify, does not appear as omnipotent and omniscient, and is capable of recognising his mistakes, which Balint showed himself able to do in some cases.[17]

The cases quoted by Balint illustrate the system he proposes. As with brief psychotherapies, these singular cases, faithfully transcribed with the questions they raise, the theoretical advances that they suggest and the description of their potential pitfalls, dead ends and successes, show the thoroughness of this research work in the field of applied psychoanalysis. Thus, case no. 24[18] in *The Doctor, His Patient and the Illness* is centred on two issues: the 'drug "doctor"', and the value and limitations of psychotherapies conducted by general practitioners. It illustrates the risks inherent in the consultant–general practitioner relationship. It stages six different protagonists: the doctor, the patient, the group, the leader, a consultant who is also the supervisor of the doctor presenting the case – whence the risk of confusion of roles – and the institution. It is the relationships among these six protagonists, confronted with the medical sphere and the circulation of the unconscious, that form the case. In the narration of this case, every little detail is important. Balint describes the reactions of each, his own attitude, his mistakes and what he perceives but does not interpret. Despite the success of the psychotherapy undertaken by the general practitioner with the help of the group, Balint leaves open the question of why he succeeds, and that of the cases where the general practitioner can enter into the process of psychotherapy. This is a long way from the cases where the issue is to deliver a fragment of knowledge, or sometimes even to use a case to illustrate a theory 'at all costs'. From the outset, Balint shows the complexity of the above-mentioned case. It is the case of a difficult patient. But the difficulties of the case reported by the doctor combine with other difficulties that are just as great. At the time when the doctor presented this patient, the group was in a critical phase in its evolution. The debate on psychotherapies run by general practitioners was creating divisions and upheavals in the Tavistock Clinic. Certain doctors were experiencing a crisis with respect to their professional identity and their caregiver ideal. Movements of rivalry with the psychiatrist consultant were considerable. In addition, the case presented by the doctor and the therapeutic success that was hoped for had social and narcissistic implications, since the patient was well known in the sector, and this doctor was just beginning to gain a clientele. Balint points out these different aspects, and shows how they appear in the group. The 'triangular crisis' between the doctor talking about his patient, his consultant, the group and its leader makes up the central issue in this case. This crisis is probably a displacement of the crisis between the doctor, his patient and his illness, the basis for all the cases presented in the groups. There is no analysis in terms of group dynamics, but Balint does note that this case enabled a maturing process in the group, leading it to overcome the crisis. There is also a maturing of the doctor presenting the case, parallel to that of the group, the elaboration of his counter-transference, his unconscious positions and the improvement in the patient's condition. Rather than using indicators of group dynamics to identify its crisis, understand it and overcome it, Balint bases himself on the shared experience of the leader and the group generated by the deadlocked doctor–patient relationship. He refers to the 'collusion of anonymity', the 'dilution of responsibility' and the 'perpetuation of the teacher–pupil relationship'. These are concepts derived from experiences in the Balint groups. When the patient's offers are not heard, and are an enigma for the doctor, the doctor can no longer take on the responsibility of the medical follow-up. He increasingly resorts to specialists and other professionals, and decisions which are sometimes far-reaching are made without anyone feeling fully responsible. The persistence of the teacher–pupil relationship is a concern that was already present in relation to the psychoanalytic cure and the training of psychoanalysts. General practitioners consider specialists to be more competent, and they submit, although with a degree of ambivalence, to their knowledge and word. Beyond their descriptive and phenomenological aspects, these concepts refer back to the notion of the 'confusion of tongues'[19] propounded by Ferenczi, and which Balint takes up again in *The Doctor, His Patient and the Illness*. Following on from his writings on the psychoanalytic cure, in medical practice the 'confusion of tongues' arises from an inadequate or unsuitable response by the doctor to the patient's offers: each is talking a language that is not understood and seemingly incomprehensible by the other. The patient complies artificially with the language used by the doctor. The mismatch between the patient's offer and the doctor's responses, and the absence of a common language between them, also have an effect on the functioning of the caregivers catering for the patient. The 'collusion of anonymity', the 'dilution of responsibility' and the 'perpetuation of the teacher–pupil relationship' reflect the difficulty for doctors in finding a language that is genuinely understood by the patient, and the fact that general practitioners conform in artificial and ambivalent manner to what is decreed by specialists, just as the patient sometimes conforms to the language used by his analyst. By using these concepts to understand the case and enable the evolution of the group and the doctors, Balint places the risk of the 'confusion of tongues', and the way to overcome it, at the centre of the training system.

Another important concept proposed by Balint is that of the 'apostolic function' of the doctor.[20] This brings the doctor's ideals into play, and his relationship with his main referents, his objects of desire, his values, his identity references and his processes of identification with the patient and his family. Because of his position as a caregiver, which confronts him with illness and what it brings into play in relation to life and death, work on the apostolic function concerns a very large part of the doctor's personality: the relationship with Lack, with the Real, with ideals and with objects that cause desire. Although this is not said specifically in these terms by Balint, reflection on the apostolic function introduces an ethical dimension. Ethics, which should be distinguished from morality or deontology, is an operation of the mind concerning not the existence of an idea or a thing, but its value, that is to say its degree of perfection in relation to a given end.[21] It is at the heart of medical practice and inherent in it. The doctor uses it constantly in implicit manner. The ethical procedure, which is an attempt to put this into words when a conflict of values arises placing the doctor in difficulty, recalls the doctor's 'apostolic function'. The Balint group, by triggering the 'apostolic function', enables the unveiling of conflicts of values, and thus generates ethical reflection.

Balint's theory on illness

Balint was more interested in the doctor–patient–illness relationship than in the genesis of the illness. Nevertheless, his elaborations on the moment of 'creation' of the illness, linked to the theory of the 'basic fault' and the primitive object-relationship, are tinged with certain psychosomatic concerns. In *The Basic Fault* he hypothesises that the withdrawal of the subject into the 'area of creation' could favour the genesis of the illness, and in *The Doctor, His Patient and the Illness* he suggests that 'during the initial "unorganized" period of their illness [. . .] people gradually withdraw from their environment and first create and then grow the illness on their own, out of themselves'. Since there is no other, nor any transference, when the subject is in the area of creation, it is difficult for a psychoanalyst to gain access to what is happening in the psyche. Balint can therefore only hypothesise on the way in which the illness forms. At the same time – and this is not a contradiction for Balint – he also hypothesises[22] that there is a psychosomatic predisposition of the individual which is rooted in the 'basic fault'. This could favour the 'basic illness'. And Balint adds:

> The 'basic fault' in the biological structure of the individual involves in varying degrees both his mind and his body [. . .]. The vestiges of his early experiences contribute to what is called his constitution, his individuality, or his character make-up, both in the psychological and in the biological sense.[23]

The way in which the doctor's responses to the patient's offers influence the course of the illness could be a return to the primitive object relationship and its difficulties. Balint's hypotheses seem rather imprecise. According to him there is regression into the area of creation and generation of illness in certain cases of psychic vulnerability, linked to a maladapted early object-relationship. The concept of the basic illness is based on a monistic conception in line with that of Ferenczi, and coherent with Balint's elaborations on 'primary love' and the 'primary substances' period.[24] He also makes implicit reference to the notion of temperament, which is a concept of medical origin[25] going back to Hippocrates, and has always remained closely linked to the sphere of medicine. By placing the genesis of the illness in a very archaic area of the psyche, Balint also adheres to an evolutionist theory. But unlike others, and in particular the Paris school,[26] he gives no definition of a psychosomatic nosography differentiating various clinical entities on the basis of a classification of mentalisations, where one end of the scale could correspond to organisations in which the psyche appears more elaborated, and the other to organisations of the psyche that are incomplete. This is also a long way from the idea of 'operative thought' as defined by Marty.[27] The area of creation, even if it is difficult to put into words, is also the area where the creativity of the individual and artistic creation originate. Although it is not well defined, we can wonder if it is not rather related to instinct and the intimate sphere, where the psyche is not separate from the body.

The development of Balint groups

Balint's theory on the doctor–patient–illness relationship, which was very pragmatic and open, has enabled analysts with various theoretical references to call on it. In France, Balint worked with analysts such as G. Raimbault and P. Benoit, who were both members of the Freudian school created by Lacan. The former was also an INSERM researcher (INSERM being the main medical research body in France, and on this account working in hospital environments) and the latter a paediatrician who became a psychoanalyst and above all a clinician. M. Sapir, with whom Balint also worked, laid the foundations for a broad, 'ecumenical' training course in medical psychology and the patient–caregiver relationship where Balint's contributions can be seen, as well as those of the group theory, psychodrama, role play and relaxation techniques that he developed. In England, Balint group leaders from the Tavistock Clinic such as R. Gosling and P. Turquet, who also worked with Balint, developed a conception of the group centred on training rather than on the training–research combination. They used Bion's contributions on group dynamics.[28] This led to a conception that differed from Balint, centred more on postgraduate education and an unequal relationship between leader and doctors. J. Salinsky and P. Sackin, for their part, describe work in a Balint group where the main question was understanding 'the nature of doctors' defences occurring in the reported cases'.[29] In Croatia, where there was considerable development of Balint groups (Croatia was perhaps among the first countries in the world to introduce Balint seminars as an official part of the education of family doctors), the work appears to have centred on 'the role of Balint Groups in the development of participants' ego'.[30] The fact that 'Balint group' became a

generic term to refer to any group centred on the patient–caregiver relationship does, however, introduce a degree of confusion. Groups working in a
psychosocial perspective aiming to improve communication between doctor
and patient have also called themselves Balint groups. Their effect on the
practice of clinicians was sometimes evaluated in standardised manner.[31]
These approaches follow on from those of Gosling and Turquet, for whom
Balint groups were above all intended to respond to 'the need for the reporting
general practitioner to maintain an appropriate psychological distance between
himself and his patients'. They also follow on from Balint's own attempts to
evaluate,[32] although these were in more standardised form and used modern
research methods. These studies, which appear to have only distant links with
Balint's theories, are nevertheless in some cases to be found on the International
Balint Federation website. The work by Kjeldmand[33] was recently presented at
the Stockholm International Conference. This is a reflection of the present-day
misapprehensions of the Balint group theories, and of the fact that many of
Balint's elaborations, in particular on the object-relationship, have been
forgotten. Some of Balint's ideas, such as the effects of the doctor's response
on the patient's illness, are being rediscovered today in psychosocial or medical
anthropology studies. The most prestigious of all medical journals, *The
Lancet*,[34] recently published an article reporting research on medical beliefs
and practices which 'discovers' that the response of the doctor influences the
patient's somatisations, and the escalation of consultations, complementary
examinations and even therapeutic proposals. This article has appeared at a
time when all the Western world is trying to rationalise the care offer, not
always in constructive manner. *The Doctor, His Patient and the Illness* is cited
in the bibliography. Appearing at the same time as the publication of several
articles assessing the effects of Balint groups, the article in *The Lancet*
concludes that there is a need for better training of doctors in the doctor–patient
relationship via a bio-psycho-social approach with a view to the rationalisation
of care. More than twenty years ago, Sapir[35] wrote that Balint's method was
addressed to only a minority of doctors (10 per cent), and that while this
method was valid for all categories of caregivers, it would be difficult to assess
its impact on medicine and society. He added:

> One of the successful roles of the group was the 'de-ideologisation' of
> medical attitudes, and the breaking away from the apostolic function
> [. . .] Might not the state, or rather the administration, in the face of budget
> problems, try to impose Balint Groups so as to make savings, thus
> destroying all their meaning?

Without adopting a perspective focused on the economic rationalisation of
care, a recent Israeli article nevertheless stresses the fallout in the health system

from Balint groups: 'Balint activity helps the facilitation of a dialogue between mental health professionals and primary care physicians [. . .] Balint groups [. . .] can be seen as an effective method to improve primary care and mental health cooperation.'[36]

At this later stage, what are the effects of Balint groups on the practice of doctors, and what is their relevance today? It is difficult to get a clear and exhaustive picture. There are several difficulties. First, Balint's theories were elaborated in a period in the exercise of medicine that is now 'dated', from both a social and a scientific viewpoint, that is to say the 1950–60 period. The paradigms on which present-day medicine is based (cellular rather than anatomo-pathological biology), and the progress in therapy and diagnosis have considerably altered approaches to illness, and the expectations and representations of doctors and patients. The place of medicine in society has altered, as has that of psychoanalysis. Despite these differences, however, concepts such as the medical sphere as an archaic object for the psyche (which says nothing about psychosomatic theory), the apostolic function, the 'drug "doctor"', the 'collusion of anonymity', the 'dilution of responsibility' and the 'flash' technique are all still relevant, as is the organisation proposed. It is, however, important to take account of evolutions in medicine, so as to avoid resorting to atemporal models. Second, despite their value, Balint groups have encountered difficulties.

Sapir[37] describes some of them from his own practice. The effects of the groups can be contradictory. Some practitioners, in counter-phobic mode, and absorbed in processes of idealisation and identification that have reached a dead end, become activists and proselytisers, heading an 'anti-academic and anti-institution crusade'. Others become psychotherapists 'at fixed times' (*à heure fixe* in the words of Sapir), and are unable to get beyond a static iden-tification with the leader and an alienation from the ideals of psychoanalysis, which generates a partitioned mode of functioning: psychotherapist at some times, doctor at others. Others again, caught up in regression movements and the constant need for anaclisis, are unable to leave the group, so that it lives on indefinitely until it finally ceases to exist on account of the departure of too many participants.[38] There are many different reasons for these difficulties, and Sapir analyses a few. Balint groups only address a minority of doctors, and it can be added that as they are liable to shift their focus in their profes-sional practice, defensive patterns can develop, as in any group feeling that they are a minority and at odds with the identity landmarks of others: 'we are not understood', 'we understand each other perfectly', 'we need to make others understand what we have gained'. The absence of any group theory could foster ritualised repetitions and the absence of elaborations on their regressive movements, resulting in difficulty in stopping them. Finally, there could be confusion between the psychotherapeutic effects of the medical

consultation, on which it is important to work, and the process of psychotherapy proper. This aspect appears very important. Indeed, Balint's desire to
create a psychotherapy specific to general practitioners (despite his warnings
and cautions and the fact that he had second thoughts on the idea of psychotherapeutic interviews cut off from daily practice), the weight of the hopes
embodied by psychoanalysis in society, and the professional identity crisis
among numerous practitioners wishing to participate in Balint groups, are all
elements that have favoured a psychotherapeutic ideal that artificially shifts
the focus of practitioners. A crisis in professional identity may motivate application to participate in a group, or else may become apparent or accentuate in
the course of group sessions. A crisis of this sort is linked to the relationships
that each doctor entertains with himself and his professional ideal, but also to
the difficulty inherent in the exercise of medicine in society, and in the way in
which society broaches this question. Is not the ideal of practitioners all the
more pervasive when there is a difficulty managing the 'apostolic function'?
Balint groups may not enable sufficient 'de-ideologisation' of those participating, generating the temptation to replace the medical ideal by a psycho-
analytic ideal. Sapir rejects any idea of a 'Balint model', and is in favour of
the development of a brand of medical psychology in which the Balint
method could be prominent, so long as it is not exclusive and can be modified
via experience acquired. 'The fact that the leader is unlike the other members
of the group, not foreign, nor identical to the trainee',[39] could favour more
flexible identifications. It seems to me that is would also foster psychic work
on relationships towards difference, otherness and what is foreign, and on the
right balance to be struck between too great resemblance and too great for-
eignness. This is very important in the caregiving relationship, in particular in
the case of disability or serious illness. Sapir also stresses the attention that
needs to be paid to the bodily dimension in practitioner training groups. This
dimension is very important, so long as due attention is given to the many
effects produced by bodily ills on the patient and on his entourage who are
faced with the Real[40] in the case of disability or serious somatic illness. This
destabilises the subjective and professional identity of doctors and caregivers.
It means that working on the 'apostolic function' is all the more important.

What can Balint groups contribute today?

Balint groups can concern doctors and caregivers wherever they are practising,
and whether or not they are working together in the same institutions. The
Balint group is not solely a group for analysing practice, nor is it merely a
peer group for exchanging experiences, nor a group for raising awareness
towards human relationships. It is different from caregiver talking-groups, in
that it places the medical sphere as a psychic object at the centre of reflection,

rather than the patient–caregiver relationship. To practitioners, it proposes work on his unconscious, in the here-and-now of the dealings with the patient, so as to enable him to progressively acquire more freedom and psychic mobility in the doctor–patient–illness relationship. Caregivers can expect 'a considerable though limited change in their personality', that is to say that they will be more at ease with their caregiving functions, and freer in relation both to their training and professional ideal, and to the way in which they engage in the relationship with the patient and his entourage. By participating regularly in the group, they experience the fact that they can relinquish the desire to know, control and understand everything. They gain greater awareness of their unconscious implications in the relationship, their reluctance or attraction towards certain things, the origins of their uneasiness towards certain patients or situations, and their identifications. They will also question themselves on their ideals, and the inevitable gap between ideals and reality, which will help them to accept their limitations and those of others. Attention to the patient's body and the effects it produces is part of the work required on the doctor–patient–illness relationship, and it confronts each individual with his caregiving identity. The continuity of the group shows that the relationship with patients is not constructed once and for all, but that it evolves. The group, in the course of its sessions, is a witness to the history of the caregiver confronted with a patient, his illness and his evolution. It forms the memory of these different histories. The experience of group movements (for instance, the feeling that there is too great a difference or too great a resemblance among participants, or between participants and others) and of the group's links with the reported cases or the institutional setting (if the group is run in a particular department) enables a softening of over-rigid identifications and favours a maturing process. It is important for the analyst in charge of the group – who should not lose sight of the psychic reality and transference – to be aware of present-day medical issues, caregivers' modes of thinking and the conditions of their practice, because it is often from day-to-day realities and the small details of the cases presented that the more general and essential questions are raised. This familiarity with the realities of practice will also avoid him making misjudged interventions, or dismissing any difficulty encountered by caregivers as internal conflicts (even if they may of course exist).

Notes

1 For further detail on the history of the Balint movement, see R. Gelly, 'Aspects théoriques du mouvement Balint' in *L'expérience Balint, histoire, actualité* (Paris: Dunod, 1982), pp. 32–76; M. Moreau-Ricaud, *Michael Balint: le renouveau de l'école de Budapest* (Ramonville Saint-Agne: Erès, 2000).

2 See Moreau-Ricaud, *Michael Balint: le renouveau de l'école de Budapest*.
3 M. Balint, *American Journal of Psychoanalysis* 62(1) (2002): 7–15.
4 M. Balint, *The Doctor, His Patient and the Illness* (London: Churchill Livingstone, 2000); M. Balint, 'Training general practitioners in psychotherapy', *British Medical Journal* 1 (1954): 115–20; M. Balint, 'Training medical students in psychotherapy', *The Lancet* (1957): 1015–18; M. Balint, E. Balint, R. Gosling and P. Hildebrand, *A Study of Doctors* (London: Tavistock Publications, 1966).
5 In Balint *et al.*, *A Study of Doctors*, the advert to recruit doctors for Balint groups differed slightly: 'Discussion Group Seminar on Psychological Problems in General Practice'.
6 *Ibid.*
7 See Chapter 2 in this book.
8 See Chapters 3 and 4 in this book.
9 For Balint, *The Doctor, His Patient and the Illness*, and for research on the flash technique.
10 Balint, 'Training general practitioners in psychotherapy', *British Medical Journal*.
11 *Ibid.* and in Balint *et al.*, *A Study of Doctors*.
12 *Ibid.*
13 Since then, there have been numerous attempts to include Balint-type trainings in medical curricula, particularly in France. The experiment conducted in the medical Faculty in Bobigny (Paris) in the 1970s was a pilot enterprise.
14 This text appeared in the *International Journal of Psychoanalysis* 47 (1966): 54–62 and was preceded by two lectures.
15 Balint, *The Doctor, His Patient and the Illness*. For M. Sapir, in 'Le groupe Balint, passé et avenir' in *L'expérience Balint: histoire et actualité*, pp. 162–98, the narration of a case should be considered as 'a dream sequence in the filiation of the previous cases'.
16 See Chapter 4 in this book.
17 See Balint, *The Doctor, His Patient and the Illness*, case no. 6, Chapter 3, and case no. 24, Chapter 15.
18 *Ibid.*, Chapter 15.
19 See the article by Ferenczi, but also the texts by Balint on the non-operative language of the analyst in certain cases.
20 For the definition of the 'apostolic function', see Chapter 4 in this book.
21 A. Lalande, *Dictionnaire de philosophie* (Paris: PUF, 1991).
22 In Balint, *The Doctor, His Patient and the Illness*.
23 *Ibid.*, pp. 255–6.
24 See Chapter 2 in this book.
25 P. Pichot, 'Histoire du concept de tempérament', *Revue Internationale de Psychopathologie* 17 (1995): 5–24.
26 P. Marty, *Mouvements individuels de vie et de mort* (Paris: Payot, 1976).
27 *Ibid.*
28 R. Gosling and P. Turquet, 'The training of general practitioners'. This text was published in a collective work, R. Gosling, D. H. Miller, P. M. Turquet and D. Woodhouse, *The Use of Small Groups in Training* (London: Codicote Press, 1967), pp. 13–75, in Balint's lifetime.
29 J. Salinsky and P. Sackin, *What Are You Feeling, Doctor?* (Abingdon: Radcliffe Medical Press, 2000).
30 M. Kulenovic and S. Blaekovic-Milakovic, 'Balint groups as a driving force for ego development', *Collegium Antropologicum* 24 (Suppl. 1) (2000): 103–8.

31 Among studies of this type, the following can be quoted: R. L. Hulsman, W. J. Ros, J. A. Winnubst and J. M. Bensing, 'Teaching clinically experienced physicians communication skills: A review of evaluation studies', *Medical Education* 33 (1999): 655–8; D. Kjeldmand, I. Holmström and U. Rosenqvist, 'Balint training makes GPs thrive better in their job', *Patient Education and Counseling* 55 (2004): 230–5; C. D. Brock and A. H. Johnson, 'Balint group observations: The white knight and other physician roles', *Family Medicine* 31 (1999): 404–8; K. P. Cataldo, K. Peeden, M. E. Geesey and L. Dickerson, 'Association between Balint training and physician empathy and work satisfaction', *Family Medicine* 37 (2005): 328–31; H. J. Dokter, H. J. Duivenvoorden and F. Verhage, 'Changes in the attitude of general practitioners as a result of participation in a Balint group,' *Family Practice* 3 (1986): 155–63; A. H. Johnson, C. D. Brock and W. J. Hueston, 'Resident physicians who continue Balint training: A longitudinal study 1982–99', *Family Medicine* 35 (2003): 428–33; D. Clarke and J. Coleman, 'Balint groups: Examining the doctor–patient relationship', *Australian Family Physician* 31 (2002): 41–4; B. Luban-Plozza, 'Empowerment techniques: From doctor-centred (Balint approach) to patient-centred discussion groups', *Patient Education and Counseling* 26(1–3) (1995): 257–63.
32 See Balint *et al.*, *A Study of Doctors*.
33 See note 31.
34 J. M. Bensing and P. F. M. Verhaak, 'Somatisation: A joint responsibility of doctor and patient', *The Lancet* 367 (2006): 452–54.
35 'Le groupe Balint, passé et avenir' in *L'expérience Balint: histoire et actualité*, pp. 162–98.
36 S. Rabin, B. Maoz, Y. Shorer and A. Matalon, 'Balint groups as "shared care" in the area of mental health in primary medicine', *Mental Health in Family Medicine* 6(3) (2009): 139–43.
37 Sapir, 'Le groupe Balint, passé et avenir' in *L'expérience Balint: histoire et actualité*. See also M. Sapir, *La formation psychologique du médecin* (Paris: Payot, 1972) and *Soignant-soigné: le corps à corps* (Paris: Payot, 1980).
38 In 1967 Turquet and Gosling (see note 28) signalled that a 'post Balint' ongoing seminar had been running for thirteen years in the Tavistock Clinic. There may have been, they say, 'a need on the part of the doctor for constant support'.
39 Sapir, unlike Balint, talks of trainer and trainee.
40 In the Lacanian sense.

Conclusion

In relation to the founding of psychoanalysis, Balint is part of the third generation. He follows on from Ferenczi, who himself entertained tumultuous relations with the 'founding father'. This distance from the origins of psychoanalysis, and his very ecumenical way of thinking, enabled Balint to explore new theories and to take an interest in the impact of psychoanalysis outside the field of the classic psychoanalytic cure.

His writings, predominantly pragmatic and clinical, do not provide a reference theory, but they illustrate a mode of thinking, and the need to breathe life into psychoanalytical thought and have it progress, accommodating both its wealth and its failings.

Thus reading Balint is above all an encouragement to avoid becoming enclosed in the sphere of the psychoanalytic cure and that of neuroses, and to elaborate tools enabling psychoanalysis to extend its models and provide contributions in other disciplines. However, this broadening does not equate with dilution or loss of specificity. The path is narrow, and requires thoroughness and discipline.

Biographical landmarks

Michael Balint was born in December 1896 in Hungary, and he died on 31 December 1970 in the UK.

His father, Doctor Bergsmann, was a general practitioner of Jewish origin. Michael Balint's original name was Mihàly Bergsmann.

He obtained a Doctorate in Medicine in 1920. In 1921, he married Alice Székely-Kovacs, a psychoanalyst with training in ethnology, and he collaborated with her professionally.

He converted to Unitarianism and changed his family name in the period 1916–25 (the actual date is not known).

From 1919 he took an interest in psychoanalysis, and attended lectures by Ferenczi. In 1924 he was awarded a Science Doctorate (physics, chemistry and biology) in Berlin while at the same time pursuing his psychoanalytic training. When he returned to Hungary in 1924 he was a recognised analyst.

With Ferenczi, he took part in the creation and development of the Budapest Polyclinic (1931). He succeeded Ferenczi as its director, and headed the facility until he left for England to flee Nazism in 1939. The same year saw the sudden death of his wife.

In 1945 he was awarded a Master of Science degree with a thesis on genetic psychology, a short version of which was published in *Problems of Human Pleasure and Behaviour*.[1]

In London he married Enid Eichholtz with whom he subsequently worked. She initiated groups of social workers who were to take on psychotherapies for couples and families (the Family Discussion Bureau). These served as a basis for reflection on the Balint groups. Enid Balint also worked with Balint on the training of doctors. The first Balint groups appeared between 1948 and 1950. Balint was working in the Tavistock Clinic (a consultant in 1949, and then with an official research post from 1952). He left the Tavistock Clinic in 1960 when he retired.

In Britain, Balint took part in debates in the British Psychoanalytical Society, where he was part of the Middle Group, or the group of independents.

He was later the scientific secretary of the Society, and elected President in 1969.

In 1955 he was elected President of the medical section of the British Psychology Society, and in 1957, with Enid Balint, he became associate professor in Cincinnati University, USA. After retiring he was in charge of postgraduate training seminars in University College Hospital, London.

Note

1 M. Balint, 'Individual differences of behaviour in early infancy and an objective method for recording them' in *Problems of Human Pleasure and Behaviour* (New York: Liveright, 1956), pp. 125–49, first published in the *Journal of Genetic Psychology* 73 (1948): 57–117.

Index